KINGSFORD®

★ ★ ★ ★   ★ ★ ★ ★

America's
BEST
BBQs

★ ★ ★ ★ ★ ★ ★ ★ ★ ★ ★ ★ ★ ★

Publications International, Ltd.
Favorite Brand Name Recipes at www.fbnr.com

Photography by Sacco Productions Limited/Chicago.
Photographers: Tom O'Connell, Peter Walters, Peter Ross
Photo Stylist/Production: Roberta Ellis, Melissa J. Sacco, Paula Walters
Food Stylists: Gail O'Donnell, Carol Parik
Assistant Food Stylist: Sally Grimes
Recipe Development: Dorothy Nichelson, Charlotte Walker

This edition published by:
Publications International, Ltd.
7373 N. Cicero Avenue
Lincolnwood, Illinois 60712

ISBN: 0-7853-7007-2

Manufactured in China.

Pictured on the front cover: Lemon Herbed Chicken *(page 39)* and Skewered Vegetables
(page 91).

Pictured on the back cover, clockwise from top left: Beef with Dry Spice Rub *(page 10)*,
Catfish with Fresh Corn Relish *(page 68)* and Grilled Pizza *(page 90)*.

8 7 6 5 4 3 2 1

KINGSFORD

America's
BEST
BBQs

BARBECUE BASICS

A DASH OF HISTORY

Henry Ford deserves credit for more than the Model T. His ingenuity helped create America's passion for outdoor cooking. In the early 1900s, Ford operated a northern Michigan sawmill that made wooden framing for his Model Ts. As piles of wood scraps grew, he searched for a way to make them useful. He soon learned how to chip the wood and convert it into the now familiar pillow-shaped briquets. These convenient briquets were originally sold through Ford automobile agencies and marked the beginning of the all-American tradition of barbecuing.

Ford Charcoal, later named **Kingsford®** charcoal briquets, is the original and still the number one brand sold in the nation today.

WHAT TYPE OF CHARCOAL?

Successful barbecuing starts with a good fire. Premium quality briquets, such as **Kingsford®** charcoal, help deliver a perfect fire in three ways. They light quicker so the coals are ready sooner. They burn longer to provide more cooking time. They perform consistently, bag after bag. The renewed interest in authentic charcoal cooking has spawned extra convenience and improved flavor in the types of charcoal available.

Ready to Light Charcoal Briquets: These coals are an especially good choice for midweek barbecues when time is at a premium. Products such as **Match Light®** ready to light briquets already contain just the right amount of lighter fluid to produce a quick-starting fire. Simply stack the briquets into a pyramid and light several briquets with a match. The coals will be ready in about 20 minutes. Be sure to close the bag tightly after each use.

A single-use lightable bag of charcoal, such as **BBQ Bag®,** is the convenient choice for tailgate parties or anytime grilling. Just light the bag, which is filled with enough ready to light briquets for one barbecue.

Charcoal Briquets with Mesquite Wood Chips: This is the perfect selection for cooks who enjoy the wonderful flavor of mesquite but feel uncomfortable grilling over pure mesquite charcoal, which burns hotter and less evenly than regular charcoal. For example, **Kingsford® with Mesquite** charcoal briquets are a blend of compressed charcoal briquets and mesquite chips. These briquets produce real mesquite smoke to enhance the flavor of outdoor fare.

It is important to remember that charcoal is porous and will absorb moisture. Always store briquets in a dry area, and keep the bag in a tightly closed or covered container. Charcoal that has been exposed to humidity or moisture can be more difficult to light.

SAFETY FIRST

Make sure the grill is on a solid surface and is set away from shrubbery, grass and overhangs. Also, make sure grill vents are not clogged with ashes before starting a fire. NEVER use gasoline or kerosene as a lighter fluid starter. Either one can cause an explosion. To get a sluggish fire going, do not add lighter fluid directly to hot coals. Instead, place 2 to 3 additional briquets in a small metal can, add lighter fluid, stack them on the pyramid of briquets with tongs, then light with a match. These briquets will restart the fire.

Remember that coals are hot (up to 1000°F) and that the heat transfers to the barbecue grill, grid, tools and food. Always wear heavy-duty mitts when cooking and handling grill and tools.

BUILDING PERFECT FIRES

How Much Charcoal? A 5-pound bag of **Kingsford®** charcoal contains 75 to 90 briquets; a 10-pound bag between 150 and 180; and a 20-pound bag 300 to 360 briquets. The number of briquets required for barbecuing depends on the size and type of grill and the amount of food to be prepared. Weather conditions also have an effect; strong winds, very cold temperatures or highly humid conditions increase the number of briquets needed for a good fire. As a rule, it takes about 30 briquets to grill 1 pound of meat. For example, you'll need 45 briquets to grill six 4-ounce hamburgers.

For **direct cooking,** food is placed directly over the coals. Make sure there is enough charcoal in a single layer to extend 1 to 2 inches beyond the area of the food on the grill. Pour briquets into the grill to determine the quantity needed, then stack them into a pyramid.

For **indirect cooking,** food is placed over a drip pan and the coals are banked either to one side or on both sides of the pan. This method is recommended for large cuts of meat, such as roasts, and fatty meats to eliminate flame flare-ups. Here's how to determine the number of briquets needed:

BRIQUETS NEEDED FOR INDIRECT COOKING, COVERED GRILL

	Diameter of Grill (inches)			
	26¾	22½	18½	14
Briquets needed on each side of drip pan for cooking 45 to 50 minutes	30	25	16	15
Briquets needed to be added on each side of drip pan every 45 minutes – use only regular briquets	9	8	5	4

Using Lighter Fluid: Kingsford™ Odorless charcoal lighter is formulated to meet strict air quality standards. Stack briquets into a pyramid. Use 2½ ounces of fluid per pound of briquets, then light with a match. Coals will be ready in 20 to 30 minutes, when they are about 80% ashed over. At night, they will have a noticeable reddish glow.

Using a Chimney Starter: This method is essentially failure-proof and no lighter fluid is required. First, remove the grid from the grill and set the chimney starter in the base of the grill. Then crumble a couple of sheets of newspaper and place them in the bottom portion of the chimney starter. Fill the top portion with charcoal briquets. Light the newspaper. Do not disturb the starter; coals will be ready in 20 to 30 minutes. Be sure to wear fireproof mitts when moving coals from the chimney starter into the base of the grill.

Using an Electric Starter: Nestle the electric starter in the coals. Plug the starter into a heavy-duty extension cord, then plug the cord into an outlet. After 8 to 10 minutes, when ash begins to form on the briquets, unplug the starter, remove it, and carefully set it aside. Arrange the briquets in a single layer, close together.

How Hot is the Grill? If you don't have a grill thermometer, here is a quick, easy way to estimate the temperature on the grill surface. Hold your hand, palm-side-down, just above the grid. Count "one thousand one, one thousand two," etc., until the heat is uncomfortable. If you can keep your hand in place before pulling away:

2 seconds - it's a hot fire, 375°F or more.
3 seconds - it's a medium-hot fire, 350° to 375°F.
4 seconds - it's a medium fire, 300° to 350°F.
5 seconds - it's a low fire, 200° to 300°F.

FLAVORED SMOKE

Flavored smoke, a combination of heady aromas from hardwoods and fresh or dried herbs, imparts a special flavor in barbecued foods. Outdoor cooks find it's both easy and fun to experiment with different meats and flavor combinations. Here are some suggestions for getting started:

As a general rule, a little goes a long way. Added flavorings should complement, not overpower, food's natural taste. Always soak flavorings, such as wood chunks, wood chips or herbs, in water at least 30 minutes before adding to the coals. The flavorings should smolder and smoke, not burn.

Hickory and mesquite chips or wood chunks are the most readily available flavorings. Other good choices are oak (good with heartier meats), cherry or apple wood (flavorful companions to poultry) and alder wood from the Northwest (marvelous with fish). Look for Kingsford® Heart-O-Hickory smoke chips in your store's barbecue section.

Grapevine cuttings and even shells from nuts, such as almonds, pecans or walnuts can add interesting flavor. You can also try water-soaked garlic cloves and orange or lemon peels.

Small bunches of fresh or dried herbs soaked in water can add fragrant flavor as well. Rosemary, bay leaves, oregano and tarragon, for example, can be teamed with wood chips or simply used by themselves for a new taste twist.

BARBECUE TOOLS AND ACCESSORIES

These tools will help make your barbecue cooking safer and more convenient.

Long-Handled Tongs, Basting Brush and Spatula: Moving hot coals and food around the grill, as well as basting and turning foods, can be dangerous. Select tools with long handles and hang them where you are working. You may want to purchase two pairs of tongs, one for coals and one for food.

Meat Thermometer: There is no better way to judge the doneness of meat than with a high quality meat thermometer. Always remember to insert the thermometer into the center of the largest muscle of the meat, with the point away from bone, fat or rotisserie rod.

Heavy-Duty Mitts: You will prevent many burns by safeguarding your hands with big, thick mitts. Keep them close to the barbecue so they are always handy.

Aluminum Foil Drip Pans: A drip pan placed beneath grilling meats will prevent flare-ups. The pan should be 1½ inches deep and extend about 3 inches beyond either end of the meat. The juices that collect in the drip pan may be used for a sauce or gravy. Bring drippings to a boil before using.

Water Spritzer: To quench flare-ups, keep a water-filled spray bottle near the barbecue.

Other Tools and Accessories: A charcoal chimney or electric charcoal starter is useful for starting the fire without lighter fluid. Hinged wire baskets facilitate the turning of some foods, such as fish fillets. Long skewers made of metal or bamboo are indispensable for kabobs. Bamboo skewers should be soaked in water at least 20 minutes before grilling to prevent the bamboo from burning.

DRY RUBS AND MARINADES

Dry rubs are combinations of seasonings and spices rubbed onto meat before grilling. Basic rubs often include coarsely ground black or white pepper, paprika and garlic powder. Some include mustard, brown sugar and even ground red pepper. Crushed herbs, such as sage, basil, thyme and oregano are other good choices.

Marinades, such as dry rubs, add flavor, but they also help tenderize less tender cuts of meat. Basic marinades include an acidic ingredient responsible for tenderizing—generally from wine, vinegar, soy sauce or lemon juice—combined with herbs, seasonings and oil. Fish and vegetables don't usually need tenderizing and should be marinated for only short periods of time (15 to 30 minutes). Beef, pork, lamb and chicken all benefit from being marinated for a few hours to overnight. Turn marinating foods occasionally to let the flavor infuse evenly. For safety, marinate all meats in the refrigerator. Resealable plastic bags are great to hold foods as they marinate.

Reserve some of the marinade before adding the meat. Use this reserved marinade as a baste while the meat is cooking. You can also serve marinade that has been drained from the meat as a dipping sauce. However, follow food safety practices; place marinade in a small saucepan and bring to a full boil. These precautions are necessary to prevent the cooked food from becoming contaminated with bacteria from the raw meat that may be present in the marinade.

A WORD ABOUT SAUCES

Sauces—rich and thick, savory or sweet—add delicious flavors to almost any grilled fare. Premium sauces, such as K.C. Masterpiece® Barbecue Sauce, capture real homemade taste and are a barbecue staple worth using often. Serve warmed sauce on the side for added zest. Here's how to protect the rich, deep color and spicy flavor of barbecue sauce, especially tomato- and molasses-based ones that can burn if applied too early:

For grilled steaks and chops: Baste with sauce after meat has been turned for the last time, about the last 3 minutes of grilling.

For grilled chicken: Baste with sauce the last 10 minutes; turn once.

For hot dogs and sausage: Baste with sauce the last 5 to 6 minutes.

For barbecued meats (cooked by indirect heat): Baste with sauce the last hour of cooking.

For smoked meats: Baste with sauce the last 30 to 45 minutes.

Basting sauces made from seasoned oils and butters may be brushed on throughout grilling.

BARBECUE TIPS

To keep food from sticking to the grid and make it easy to turn, brush the hot grid with vegetable oil before cooking.

To "line" your food with appetizing grill marks, allow the grid to heat thoroughly before adding the food.

To avoid flare-ups and charred food when grilling, remove visible fat from meat or cook indirectly.

Watch foods carefully during grilling. Total cooking time will vary with the type of food, position on the grill, weather, temperature of the coals and degree of doneness you desire.

Use a meat thermometer to accurately determine the doneness of large cuts of meat or poultry cooked on the rotisserie or covered grill.

Foods wrapped in foil and cooked on the grill should be turned often to prevent burning and ensure even cooking.

If you partially cook foods in a microwave or on a range, immediately finish cooking the food on the grill. Do not refrigerate partially cooked foods or let them sit at room temperature before grilling is completed.

In hot weather, food should never sit out for over 1 hour. Remember, keep hot foods hot and cold foods cold.

Always serve cooked food from the grill on a clean plate, not one that held raw food.

Always use tongs or a spatula when handling meat. Piercing meat with a fork allows delicious juices to escape and makes meat less moist.

The secret to evenly cooked vegetable kabobs is to parboil solid or starchy vegetables before they are threaded onto skewers for grilling. For best results, grill vegetables on skewers separate from meat.

If you use wooden or bamboo skewers when making kabobs, be sure to soak them in cold water at least 20 minutes before grilling.

Herb brushes lightly season barbecued foods. To make, fasten a bunch of freshly picked herb sprigs to the tip of a wooden spoon handle with kitchen twine or cotton string. Dip herb brushes in olive oil and baste whatever you're grilling. Then untie and throw the sprigs into the fire.

When barbecuing food for more than an hour, add 10 to 12 **Kingsford®** charcoal briquets around the outer edge of the fire as cooking starts. When these briquets are ready, add them to the center of the fire as needed to maintain constant temperature. Use only regular briquets (not instant lighting briquets).

Hot Off the Grill
MEATS

BEEF WITH DRY SPICE RUB

You can grill mushrooms and new potatoes on skewers over medium coals while you wait for the briquets to burn down to medium-low to cook the beef.

> **3 tablespoons firmly packed brown sugar**
> **1 tablespoon black peppercorns**
> **1 tablespoon yellow mustard seeds**
> **1 tablespoon whole coriander seeds**
> **4 cloves garlic**
> **1½ to 2 pounds beef top round steak or London Broil**
>   **(about 1½ inches thick)**
>   **Vegetable or olive oil**
>   **Salt**

Place brown sugar, peppercorns, mustard seeds, coriander seeds and garlic in a blender or food processor; process until seeds and garlic are crushed. Rub beef with oil, then pat on spice mixture. Season generously with salt.

Oil hot grid to help prevent sticking. Grill beef, on a covered grill, over medium-low Kingsford briquets, 16 to 20 minutes for medium doneness, turning once. Let stand 5 minutes before slicing. Cut across the grain into thin, diagonal slices.   *Makes 6 servings*

Grilled Mushrooms: Thread mushrooms, 1½ to 2 inches in diameter, on metal or bamboo skewers. Brush lightly with oil; season with salt and pepper. Grill 7 to 12 minutes, turning occasionally.

Grilled New Potatoes: Cook or microwave small new potatoes until barely tender. Thread on metal or bamboo skewers. Brush lightly with oil; season with salt and pepper. Grill 10 to 15 minutes, turning occasionally.

Note: Bamboo skewers should be soaked in water for at least 20 minutes to keep them from burning.

Beef with Dry Spice Rub

MEAT GRILLING POINTERS

- Turn small cuts, such as patties, chops, steaks and kabobs, halfway through grilling time.

- Turn large cuts, such as roasts, every 20 to 30 minutes.

- Check final temperature of large cuts with a meat thermometer inserted in the thickest portion of the meat. The thermometer should not touch bone or fat. Let meat stand 10 minutes on cutting board before slicing.

Meat Grilling Chart

Cut of Meat	Method/Grill	Temperature of Briquets	Grilling Time in Minutes/Doneness
Ground Beef Patties			
¾ inch	Direct/Uncovered	Medium	10 to 11/Medium
½ inch	Direct/Uncovered	Medium	7 to 10/Medium
Beef Top Round Steak			
¾ to 1 inch	Direct/Uncovered	Medium	12 to 14/Medium
1½ inches	Direct/Uncovered	Medium-Low	23 to 25/Medium
Beef Eye Round Steak			
¾ to 1 inch	Direct/Uncovered	Medium	12 to 16/Medium
Beef Rib Eye Steak or Top Loin Steak			
¾ inch	Direct/Uncovered	Medium	7 to 9/Medium
1 inch	Direct/Uncovered	Medium-Low	9 to 12/Medium
1½ inches	Direct/Uncovered	Medium-Low	21 to 24/Medium
Beef Porterhouse or T-Bone Steak			
1 inch	Direct/Uncovered	Medium	10 to 14/Medium
1½ inches	Direct/Uncovered	Medium-Low	26 to 30/Medium
Beef Tenderloin Steak			
1 inch	Direct/Uncovered	Medium	11 to 13/Medium
1½ inches	Direct/Uncovered	Medium	15 to 17/Medium
Beef Boneless Sirloin Steak			
¾ inch	Direct/Uncovered	Medium	8 to 11/Medium
2 inches	Direct/Uncovered	Medium-Low	34 to 40/Medium
Beef Flank Steak			
1½ pounds	Direct/Uncovered	Medium	12 to 15/Medium
Beef Sirloin Kabobs			
1 to 1½ inch cubes	Direct/Uncovered	Medium	8 to 11/Medium

Cut of Meat	Method/Grill	Temperature of Briquets	Grilling Time in Minutes/Doneness
Beef Bottom Round Roast			
3 to 3½ pounds	Indirect/Covered	Medium-Low	21 to 25/Rare
Beef Eye Round Roast Butterflied			
2 to 4 pounds	Direct/Covered	Medium	16 to 20/Medium
Beef Top Round Roast			
3 to 3½ pounds	Indirect/Covered	Medium-Low	23 to 27/Rare to Medium-Rare
Beef Boneless Chuck Roast			
3 to 4 pounds	Indirect/Covered	Medium-Low	25 to 30/Medium
Beef Tri-Tip Roast			
1¾ to 2 pounds	Direct/Covered	Medium	21 to 25/Medium
Beef Round Tip Roast			
5 to 8 pounds	Indirect/Covered	Medium-Low	20 to 25/Medium
Beef Tenderloin Roast			
1½ to 2 pounds	Direct/Covered	Medium	16 to 24/Medium
Pork Loin Chops			
Bone-In ¾ inch	Indirect/Covered	Medium	8 to 11/Well
Bone-In 1½ inches	Indirect/Covered	Medium	19 to 22/Well
Boneless ¾ inch	Indirect/Covered	Medium	16 to 18/Well
Boneless 1½ inches	Indirect/Covered	Medium	16 to 18/Well
Pork Kabobs			
1 inch pieces	Indirect/Covered	Medium	9 to 13/Well
Pork Tenderloin Roast			
½ to 1½ pounds	Indirect/Covered	Medium	16 to 21/Well
Lamb Loin or Rib Chops			
Bone-In 1 inch	Direct/Uncovered	Medium	9 to 10/Medium
Lamb Sirloin Steaks			
1 inch	Direct/Uncovered	Medium	9 to 10/Medium
Lamb Kabobs			
1-inch pieces	Direct/Uncovered	Medium	7 to 8/Medium
Lamb Butterflied Leg			
4 to 7 pounds	Direct/Uncovered	Medium	40 to 50/Medium

Cooking times are courtesy of National Live Stock and Meat Board, National Pork Producers Council and American Lamb Council.

PORK TENDERLOIN WITH
ORANGE GLAZE

1 cup orange juice
¼ cup cider vinegar
1 tablespoon finely grated fresh ginger
1 teaspoon finely grated orange peel
1 pork tenderloin (about 1 pound)
   Orange Glaze (recipe follows)
   Salt and black pepper

Combine orange juice, vinegar, ginger and orange peel in a shallow glass dish or large heavy plastic bag. Add pork tenderloin; cover dish or close bag. Marinate in refrigerator at least 4 hours, turning several times.

Meanwhile, prepare Orange Glaze. Reserve about ¼ cup for brushing on meat. Remove pork from marinade; discard marinade. Season pork with salt and pepper.

Oil hot grid to help prevent sticking. Grill pork, on a covered grill, over medium Kingsford briquets, 18 to 25 minutes until a meat thermometer inserted in the thickest part registers 155°F. Brush with reserved Orange Glaze the last 5 to 10 minutes of cooking. Let pork stand 5 to 10 minutes to allow the internal temperature to rise to 160°F before slicing. Slice and serve with remaining Orange Glaze. Garnish, if desired.   *Makes 4 servings*

ORANGE GLAZE

1 cup orange marmalade
1 tablespoon finely grated ginger
2 tablespoons soy sauce
2 tablespoons cider vinegar
1 tablespoon Dijon mustard
¼ teaspoon salt
¼ teaspoon black pepper

Melt orange marmalade in a small saucepan. Stir in remaining ingredients; reduce heat to low. Cook about 10 minutes. Reserve ¼ cup of glaze for brushing pork; place remaining glaze in a small bowl to serve as accompaniment. Makes about 1 cup.

Pork Tenderloin with Orange Glaze

WINE & ROSEMARY LAMB SKEWERS

    1 cup dry red wine
    ¼ cup olive oil
    3 cloves garlic, cut into slivers
    1 tablespoon chopped fresh thyme *or* 1 teaspoon
        dried thyme leaves, crumbled
    1 tablespoon chopped fresh rosemary *or* 1 teaspoon
        dried rosemary leaves, crumbled
    2 pounds boneless lamb, cut into 1-inch cubes
    Salt and black pepper
    4 or 5 sprigs fresh rosemary (optional)
    Grilled Bread (recipe follows)

Combine wine, oil, garlic, thyme and rosemary in a shallow glass dish or large heavy plastic bag. Add lamb; cover dish or close bag. Marinate lamb in the refrigerator up to 12 hours, turning several times. Remove lamb from marinade; discard marinade. Thread lamb onto 6 long metal skewers. Season to taste with salt and pepper.

Oil hot grid to help prevent sticking. Grill lamb, on a covered grill, over medium Kingsford briquets, 8 to 12 minutes, turning once or twice. Remove grill cover and throw rosemary onto coals the last 4 to 5 minutes of cooking, if desired. Move skewers to side of grid to keep warm while bread is toasting. Garnish, if desired. *Makes 6 servings*

GRILLED BREAD

    ¼ cup olive oil
    2 tablespoons red wine vinegar
    1 baguette (about 12 inches long), sliced
        lengthwise, then cut into pieces
    Salt and freshly ground black pepper

Mix oil and vinegar in cup; brush over cut surfaces of bread. Season lightly with salt and pepper. Grill bread cut side down, on an uncovered grill, over medium Kingsford briquets until lightly toasted. Makes 6 servings.

Wine & Rosemary Lamb Skewers
and Grilled Bread

SAUSAGE, PEPPERS & ONIONS
WITH GRILLED POLENTA

5 cups canned chicken broth
1½ cups Italian polenta or yellow cornmeal
1½ cups cooked fresh corn or thawed frozen corn
2 tablespoons butter or margarine
1 cup (4 ounces) freshly grated Parmesan cheese
6 Italian-style sausages
2 small to medium red onions, sliced into rounds
1 *each* medium red and green bell pepper, cored,
    seeded and cut into 1-inch-wide strips
½ cup Marsala or sweet vermouth (optional)
    Olive oil

To make polenta, bring chicken broth to a boil in a large pot. Add polenta and cook at a gentle boil, stirring frequently, for about 30 minutes. If polenta starts to stick and burn to the bottom of the pot, add up to ½ cup water. During the last 5 minutes of cooking, stir in corn and butter. Remove from heat; stir in Parmesan cheese. Transfer polenta into a greased 13×9-inch baking pan; let cool until firm and set enough to cut. (Polenta can be prepared a day ahead and held in the refrigerator.)

Prick each sausage in 4 or 5 places with a fork. Place sausages, red onions and bell peppers in a large shallow glass dish or large heavy plastic bag. Pour Marsala over food; cover dish or close bag. Marinate in refrigerator up to 4 hours, turning sausages and vegetables several times. (If you don't wish to marinate the sausages and vegetables in Marsala, just eliminate this step.)

Oil hot grid to help prevent sticking. Cut polenta into squares, then cut into triangles, if desired. Brush one side with oil. Grill polenta oil side down, on a covered grill, over medium Kingsford briquets, about 4 minutes until lightly toasted. Halfway through cooking time, brush top with oil, then turn and continue grilling. Move polenta to edge of grill to keep warm.

When coals are medium-low, drain sausage and vegetables from wine; discard wine. Grill sausage on a covered grill, 15 to 20 minutes until cooked through, turning several times. After the sausage has cooked 10 minutes, place vegetables in the center of the grid. Grill vegetables 10 to 12 minutes until tender, turning once or twice.   *Makes 6 servings*

Sausage, Peppers & Onions
with Grilled Polenta

TERIYAKI GLAZED BEEF KABOBS

1¼ to 1½ pounds beef top or bottom sirloin, cut into
    1-inch cubes
½ cup bottled teriyaki baste & glaze
1 teaspoon Oriental sesame oil (optional)
1 clove garlic, minced
8 to 12 green onions
1 or 2 plum tomatoes, cut into slices (optional)

Thread beef cubes on metal or bamboo skewers. (Soak bamboo skewers in water for at least 20 minutes to keep them from burning.) Combine teriyaki glaze, sesame oil and garlic in a small bowl. Brush beef and onions with part of the glaze, saving some for grilling; let stand 15 to 30 minutes.

Oil hot grid to help prevent sticking. Grill beef, on a covered grill, over medium Kingsford briquets, 6 to 9 minutes for medium doneness, turning several times and brushing with glaze. Add onions and tomatoes, if desired, to the grid 3 or 4 minutes after the beef; grill until onions and tomatoes are tender. Remove from grill; brush skewers, onions and tomatoes with remaining glaze.

Makes 4 servings

PORK KABOBS WITH MUSTARD–BOURBON GLAZE

1 boneless pork loin roast (1 to 1¼ pounds)
  Salt and black pepper
3 tablespoons Dijon mustard
3 tablespoons bourbon or water
¼ cup soy sauce
¼ cup firmly packed brown sugar
1 tablespoon Worcestershire sauce

Cut pork into 1-inch cubes; season with salt and pepper. Combine mustard, bourbon, soy sauce, brown sugar and Worcestershire sauce in a shallow glass dish or large heavy plastic bag. Add pork; cover dish or close bag. Marinate in refrigerator up to 4 hours. Remove pork from marinade; discard marinade. Thread pork onto metal or bamboo skewers. (Soak bamboo skewers in water for at least 20 minutes to prevent burning.)

Oil hot grid to help prevent sticking. Grill pork, on a covered grill, over medium Kingsford briquets, 8 to 12 minutes until pork is cooked through, turning once. Pork should be juicy and slightly pink in the center.

Makes 4 servings

Teriyaki Glazed Beef Kabobs

NUTTY BURGERS

1½ pounds ground beef
1 medium onion, finely chopped
1 clove garlic, minced
1 cup dry bread crumbs
⅓ cup grated Parmesan cheese
⅔ cup pine nuts
⅓ cup chopped parsley
2 eggs
1½ teaspoons salt
1 teaspoon black pepper
12 slices French bread (each ¼ inch thick) *or*
6 hamburger buns
Green onions for garnish

Combine beef, onion, garlic, bread crumbs, cheese, pine nuts, parsley, eggs, salt and pepper in a medium bowl. Shape meat mixture into 6 thick patties.

Oil hot grid to help prevent sticking. Grill patties, on a covered grill, over medium-hot Kingsford briquets, 10 minutes for medium doneness, turning once. Serve on French bread. Garnish with chopped green onion, if desired.

Makes 6 servings

BBQ BABY BACK RIBS

1 cup seasoned rice vinegar
1 cup freshly squeezed orange juice
½ cup maple syrup
½ cup water
2 tablespoons finely grated fresh ginger
2 tablespoons finely chopped fresh cilantro
4 cloves garlic, coarsely chopped
2 teaspoons Oriental sesame oil
Black pepper
1 teaspoon crushed red pepper flakes
3 to 5 pounds pork loin back ribs
1 tablespoon cornstarch
Salt

Combine vinegar, orange juice, maple syrup, water, ginger, cilantro, garlic, sesame oil, 1 teaspoon black pepper and red pepper flakes in a medium bowl. Reserve 1 cup of marinade. Place ribs in a shallow glass dish or large heavy plastic bag. Pour remaining marinade over ribs; cover dish or close bag. Marinate in refrigerator 4 to 24 hours.

To make glaze, place reserved 1 cup marinade in a small saucepan; whisk in cornstarch. Bring to a boil, stirring frequently. Boil about 30 seconds until mixture thickens, stirring constantly; set aside. Remove ribs from marinade; discard marinade.

Oil hot grid to help prevent sticking. Grill ribs, on a covered grill, over medium Kingsford briquets, 8 to 12 minutes, turning and rearranging the ribs frequently. Brush ribs with glaze the last few minutes of cooking. Remove ribs from grill; baste with glaze. *Makes 4 to 6 servings*

PORK TENDERLOIN WITH
FRESH PLUM SAUCE

Fresh Plum Sauce (recipe follows)
Oriental sesame oil
1 pork tenderloin (about 1 pound)
Salt and black pepper

Prepare Fresh Plum Sauce. Rub sesame oil into pork. Season generously with salt and pepper.

Oil hot grid to help prevent sticking. Grill pork, on a covered grill, over medium Kingsford briquets, 18 to 25 minutes until a meat thermometer inserted in the thickest part registers 155°F. Let stand 5 to 10 minutes to allow the internal temperature to rise to 160°F before slicing. Slice and serve with sauce. *Makes 4 servings*

FRESH PLUM SAUCE

1 tablespoon vegetable oil
1 tablespoon minced garlic
1 tablespoon grated or minced fresh ginger
1½ teaspoons minced jalapeño chili pepper
1 pound plums, cut into halves, pitted, chopped
½ cup sliced green onions, with tops
¼ cup firmly packed dark brown sugar or to taste
2 tablespoons soy sauce
2 tablespoons seasoned rice vinegar or apple cider vinegar
¼ cup chopped fresh cilantro

Heat oil in a medium saucepan. Add garlic, ginger and chili pepper; sauté, stirring, about 1 minute. Add all remaining ingredients except cilantro. Simmer 15 minutes, stirring frequently, until mixture has a chunky, saucelike texture. Adjust flavors to taste. Remove from heat and cool to room temperature. Stir in cilantro. Makes about 2 cups.

GRILLED SMOKED SAUSAGE

1 cup apricot or pineapple preserves
1 tablespoon lemon juice
1½ pounds smoked sausage

Heat preserves in small saucepan until melted. Strain; reserve fruit pieces. Combine strained preserve liquid with lemon juice in a small bowl.

Oil hot grid to help prevent sticking. Grill whole sausage on an uncovered grill, over low Kingsford briquets, 10 minutes. Halfway through cooking, baste with glaze, then turn and continue grilling until heated through. Remove sausage from grill; baste with glaze. Garnish with fruit pieces.
Makes 6 servings

BLUE CHEESE BURGERS
WITH RED ONIONS

These are terrific plain, but they're even better served with a spread of one part mayonnaise to one part Dijon mustard. Offer accompaniments such as sliced tomatoes and soft-leaf lettuce (Boston, bibb, butter or red leaf).

    2 pounds ground chuck
    2 cloves garlic, minced
    1 teaspoon salt
    ½ teaspoon black pepper
    4 ounces blue cheese
    ⅓ cup coarsely chopped walnuts, toasted (page 86)
    1 torpedo (long) red onion *or* 2 small red onions,
        sliced into ⅜-inch-thick rounds
    2 baguettes (each 12 inches long)
        Olive or vegetable oil

Combine beef, garlic, salt and pepper in a medium bowl. Shape meat mixture into 12 oval patties. Mash cheese and blend with walnuts in a small bowl. Divide cheese mixture equally; place onto centers of 6 meat patties. Top with remaining meat patties; tightly pinch edges together to seal.

Oil hot grid to help prevent sticking. Grill patties and onions, if desired, on a covered grill, over medium Kingsford briquets, 7 to 12 minutes for medium doneness, turning once. Cut baguettes into 4-inch lengths; split each piece and brush cut side with olive oil. Move cooked burgers to edge of grill to keep warm. Grill bread, oil side down, until lightly toasted. Serve burgers on toasted baguettes.   *Makes 6 servings*

GRILLED PORK TENDERLOIN
WITH MUSTARD SAUCE

    1 pork tenderloin roast (about 1½ pounds)
        Salt and black pepper to taste
    ¾ cup dry white wine
    1 tablespoon minced onion
    ¾ cup chicken broth
    ½ cup whipping cream
    3 tablespoons Dijon mustard
    1 teaspoon freshly squeezed lemon juice
        Chopped parsley for garnish

Season pork with salt and pepper. Oil hot grid to help prevent sticking. Grill pork, on a covered grill, over medium-hot Kingsford briquets, 20 to 25 minutes until meat thermometer inserted into thickest portion registers 155°F, turning once or twice.

Combine wine and onion in skillet. Boil rapidly 3 to 4 minutes to reduce mixture to 2 tablespoons. Whisk in broth and cream; bring to boil. Simmer 2 to 3 minutes until mixture thickens slightly. Whisk in mustard to blend. Season to taste with salt and lemon juice. Cut pork into ½-inch-thick slices. Serve with mustard sauce. Garnish with chopped parsley.

Makes 4 to 6 servings

Blue Cheese Burgers with Red Onions

PORK CHOPS WITH ORANGE–RADISH RELISH

2 cups orange juice
⅓ cup lime juice
⅓ cup firmly packed brown sugar
3 medium oranges, peeled, seeded and cut into
  ¼-inch pieces
¼ cup chopped red onion
¼ cup diced radishes
2 tablespoons finely chopped fresh cilantro
6 pork chops (about ¾ inch thick)
  Salt and black pepper
  Orange curls and radishes for garnish

Combine both juices and brown sugar in a saucepan. Cook mixture at a low boil about 20 minutes until reduced to about ½ cup and it has a syruplike consistency, stirring often. Set aside ¼ cup of sauce for basting.

Meanwhile, prepare Orange-Radish Relish by combining oranges, onion, and diced radishes in a colander or strainer and drain well; transfer to a bowl. Add cilantro and gently stir in remaining orange syrup. Season pork with salt and pepper.

Oil hot grid to help prevent sticking. Grill pork, on a covered grill, over medium Kingsford briquets, 7 to 10 minutes. (Pork is done at 160°F; it should be juicy and still slightly pink in the center.) Halfway through cooking, brush with reserved ¼ cup orange syrup and turn once. Serve with Orange-Radish Relish. Garnish with orange curls and radishes.

Makes 6 servings

WINE COUNTRY STEAK

½ cup olive oil
  Juice of 1 lime or lemon
1 cup Cabernet, Merlot or other dry red wine
¼ cup soy sauce
3 cloves garlic, minced or pressed
1½ tablespoon Dijon mustard
1 teaspoon black pepper
1 beef flank steak (about 2 pounds), pounded to
  about ½ inch thick

Whisk together oil, lime juice, wine, soy sauce, garlic, mustard and pepper in a medium bowl. Place beef in a shallow glass dish or large heavy plastic bag; pour marinade over beef. Cover dish or close bag. Marinate in refrigerator 12 to 24 hours, turning once or twice. Remove beef from marinade; discard marinade.

Oil grid to help prevent sticking. Grill beef, on a covered grill, over medium Kingsford briquets, 6 to 8 minutes for rare doneness; 9 to 12 minutes for medium-rare doneness, turning once or twice. Cut across grain into thin, diagonal slices.

Makes 6 servings

Pork Chops with Orange-Radish Relish

BEEF TENDERLOIN WITH DIJON–CREAM SAUCE

Beef tenderloin roasts can be purchased in different weights, depending on how they are cut out of the tenderloin. The tenderloin is elongated with a rounded large end, gradually tapering to a thin, flat end. Purchase a center-cut piece or a piece cut from the thicker end if you can, as they will grill more evenly. Allow 4 to 5 ounces of meat per serving. Test doneness with a thermometer and remove beef from the grill just before it reaches the desired temperature since the internal temperature can rise 5°F as the roast stands.

2 tablespoons olive oil
3 tablespoons balsamic vinegar*
1 beef tenderloin roast (about 1½ to 2 pounds)
　Salt
1½ tablespoons white peppercorns
1½ tablespoons black peppercorns
3 tablespoons mustard seeds
　Dijon-Cream Sauce (recipe follows)

Combine oil and vinegar in a cup; rub onto beef. Season generously with salt. Let stand 15 minutes.

Meanwhile, coarsely crush peppercorns and mustard seeds in a blender or food processor or by hand with a mortar and pestle. Roll beef in crushed mixture, pressing it into the surface to coat.

Oil hot grid to help prevent sticking. Grill beef, on a covered grill, over medium Kingsford briquets, 16 to 24 minutes (depending on size and thickness) until a meat thermometer inserted in the center almost registers 150°F for medium-rare. (Cook until 160°F for medium or 170°F well-done; add another 5 minutes for every 10°F.) Turn halfway through cooking. Let stand 5 to 10 minutes before slicing. Slice and serve with a few spoonfuls of sauce. *Makes 6 servings*

*Substitute 2 tablespoons red wine vinegar *plus* 1½ teaspoons sugar for the balsamic vinegar.

DIJON–CREAM SAUCE

1 can (14½ ounces) beef broth
1 cup whipping cream
2 tablespoons butter, softened
1½ to 2 tablespoons Dijon mustard
1 to 1½ tablespoons balsamic vinegar*
　Coarsely crushed black peppercorns and mustard
　　seeds for garnish

Bring beef broth and whipping cream to a boil in a saucepan. Boil gently until reduced to about 1 cup; sauce will be thick enough to coat a spoon. Remove from heat; stir butter, a little at a time, until all the butter is melted. Stir in mustard and vinegar, adjusting amounts to taste. Sprinkle with peppercorns and mustard seeds. Makes about 1 cup.

*Substitute 2 teaspoons red wine vinegar *plus* 1 teaspoon sugar for the balsamic vinegar.

Beef Tenderloin with Dijon-Cream Sauce

LONDON BROIL DIJON

2 tablespoons olive or vegetable oil
2 large heads garlic, separated into cloves and
    peeled
1 can (14½ ounces) low-salt beef broth
½ cup water
1 sprig fresh oregano or parsley
1½ tablespoons Dijon mustard
2 pound beef top round steak or London Broil
    (about 1½ inches thick)
Salt and black pepper

Heat oil in a medium saucepan; add garlic and sauté over medium-low heat, stirring frequently, until garlic just starts to brown in spots. Add broth, water and oregano. Simmer until mixture is reduced by about one third. Process broth mixture, in batches, in blender or food processor until smooth. Return to the saucepan; whisk in mustard. Set aside. Season meat with salt and pepper.

Oil hot grid to help prevent sticking. Grill beef, in a covered grill, over medium-low Kingsford briquets, 10 to 14 minutes for medium-rare doneness; 12 to 16 minutes for medium doneness, turning once or twice. Let stand 5 minutes before slicing. Cut across grain into thin, diagonal slices. Gently rewarm sauce and serve as accompaniment.   *Makes 6 servings*

LAMB WITH FRESH MINT VINAIGRETTE

1½ cups firmly packed mint leaves
½ cup firmly packed parsley leaves
1 clove garlic, chopped
⅓ cup olive oil
¼ cup white or red wine vinegar
2 to 4 teaspoons sugar
Salt
Black pepper
8 lamb loin chops (about 4 ounces each)
Additional salt and freshly ground black pepper

Place mint, parsley, garlic, oil, vinegar, 2 teaspoons sugar, ½ teaspoon salt and ¼ teaspoon pepper into a blender or food processor; process until mixture is smooth and thickened. Adjust sugar and salt to taste. Season lamb with salt and pepper.

Oil hot grid to help prevent sticking. Grill lamb, on a covered grill, over medium Kingsford briquets, 6 to 9 minutes for medium doneness, turning once. Serve sauce with lamb.   *Makes 4 servings*

PORK ROAST WITH HONEY–MUSTARD GLAZE

*Pork that is smoked over fruit woods or mesquite has a milder
smoky flavor than hickory.*

Wood chunks or chips for smoking
$\frac{1}{3}$ cup honey
$\frac{1}{4}$ cup whole-seed or coarse-grind prepared mustard
    Grated peel and juice of 1 medium orange
 1 teaspoon minced fresh ginger *or* $\frac{1}{4}$ teaspoon
    ground ginger
$\frac{1}{2}$ teaspoon salt
$\frac{1}{8}$ teaspoon ground red pepper
    Apple juice at room temperature
 1 boneless pork loin roast ($3\frac{1}{2}$ to 4 pounds)

Soak about 4 wood chunks or several handfuls of wood chips in water;
drain. Mix honey, mustard, grated orange peel and juice, ginger, salt and
pepper in small bowl.

Arrange medium-low Kingsford briquets on each side of a rectangular metal
or foil drip pan. Pour in apple juice to fill pan half full. Add soaked wood
(all the chunks; part of the chips) to the fire.

Oil hot grid to help prevent sticking. Place pork on grid directly above drip
pan. Grill pork, on a covered grill, 20 to 30 minutes per pound until a meat
thermometer inserted in thickest part registers 155°F. If your grill has a
thermometer, maintain a cooking temperature of about 300°F. Add a few
more briquets to both sides of fire every 45 minutes to 1 hour, or as
necessary, to maintain a constant temperature. Add more soaked wood
chips every 30 minutes. Brush meat with honey mustard mixture twice
during the last 40 minutes of cooking. Let pork stand 10 minutes before
slicing to allow the internal temperature to rise to 160°F. Slice and serve
with sauce made from pan drippings (directions follow), if desired.

Makes 6 to 8 servings

To make a sauce from pan drippings: Taste the liquid and drippings left in
the drip pan. If the drippings have a mild smoky flavor they will make a
nice sauce. (If a strong-flavored wood, such as hickory, or too many wood
chips were used, the drippings may be overwhelmingly smoky.) Remove
excess fat from drip pan with a bulb baster; discard. Measure liquid and
drippings; place in a saucepan. For each cup of liquid, use 1 to
2 tablespoons cider vinegar and 2 teaspoons cornstarch mixed with a little
cold water until smooth. Stir vinegar-cornstarch mixture into saucepan.
Stirring constantly, bring to a boil over medium heat and boil 1 minute.
Makes 6 to 8 servings.

MICRO-GRILLED PORK RIBS

1 tablespoon firmly packed brown sugar
2 teaspoons ground cumin
1 teaspoon salt
½ teaspoon black pepper
   Dash ground red pepper (optional)
3 pounds pork back ribs
⅓ cup water
½ cup K.C. Masterpiece Barbecue Sauce
   Grilled Sweet Potatoes (recipe follows)

Combine brown sugar, cumin, salt and peppers in small bowl. Rub onto ribs. Arrange ribs in single layer in 13×9-inch microwave-safe baking dish. Pour water over ribs; cover loosely with plastic wrap. Microwave on MEDIUM-HIGH (70% power) 15 minutes, rearranging ribs and rotating dish halfway through cooking time.*

Arrange medium-hot Kingsford briquets on one side of grill. Place ribs on grid area opposite briquets. Barbecue ribs, on a covered grill, 15 to 20 minutes, turning every 5 minutes and basting with sauce the last 10 minutes. Ribs should be browned and cooked through. Serve with Grilled Sweet Potatoes.   *Makes 4 servings*

*This recipe was tested in a 700-watt microwave oven. If your oven's wattage is different, the cooking time will need to be adjusted.

Grilled Sweet Potatoes or Baking Potatoes: Slice potatoes into ¼-inch-thick rounds, allowing about ⅓ pound potatoes per serving. Brush both sides of slices lightly with oil. Place on grid around edges of medium-hot Kingsford briquets. Cook potatoes, on a covered grill, 10 to 12 minutes until golden brown and tender, turning once.

BEEF WITH CHUNKY TOMATO SAUCE

1¼ cups chopped seeded tomatoes (about ¾ pound)
⅓ cup oil-packed sun-dried tomato halves, drained
2 tablespoons white wine vinegar
   Salt
½ teaspoon sugar
1 clove garlic, minced
   Black pepper
1 beef cross rib steak (about 1¼ pounds)

With a knife or in a food processor fitted with a metal blade, chop both fresh and dried tomatoes until tomatoes turn into a rough-textured sauce. Add vinegar, ½ teaspoon salt, sugar, garlic and ¼ teaspoon pepper; adjust flavors to taste. Set aside. Season beef with salt and pepper.

Oil hot grid to help prevent sticking. Grill beef, on a covered grill, over medium Kingsford briquets, 10 to 12 minutes for medium doneness, turning once. Serve with sauce.   *Makes 4 servings*

Micro-Grilled Pork Ribs and
Grilled Sweet Potatoes

GUADALAJARA BEEF

Experiment with aromatics, such as fresh herbs and citrus peel, to vary the flavor of recipes. Our suggestion is to add 2 or 3 fresh rosemary branches and the peel of half an orange directly to coals when turning meat.

    1 bottle (12 ounces) Mexican dark beer*
    ¼ cup soy sauce
    2 cloves garlic, minced
    1 teaspoon ground cumin
    1 teaspoon chili powder
    1 teaspoon hot pepper sauce
    4 beef bottom sirloin steaks or boneless tri tip
        steaks (4 to 6 ounces each)
    Salt and black pepper
    Red, green and yellow bell peppers, cut
        lengthwise into quarters, seeded (optional)
    Salsa (recipe follows)
    Flour tortillas (optional)
    Lime wedges

Combine beer, soy sauce, garlic, cumin, chili powder and hot pepper sauce in a large shallow glass dish or large heavy plastic bag. Add beef; cover dish or close bag. Marinate in refrigerator up to 12 hours, turning beef several times. Remove beef from marinade; discard marinade. Season with salt and pepper.

Oil hot grid to help prevent sticking. Grill beef and peppers, if desired, on covered grill, over medium Kingsford briquets, 8 to 12 minutes, turning once. Beef should be medium doneness and peppers tender. Serve with Salsa, tortillas if desired and lime.   *Makes 4 servings*

*Substitute any beer for the Mexican dark beer.

SALSA

    2 cups coarsely chopped seeded tomatoes (about
        1¼ pounds)
    2 green onions, with tops, sliced
    1 clove garlic, minced
    1 to 2 teaspoons minced seeded jalapeño or serrano
        chili pepper, fresh or canned
    1 tablespoon olive or vegetable oil
    2 to 3 teaspoons lime juice
    8 to 10 sprigs fresh cilantro, minced (optional)
    ½ teaspoon salt or to taste
    ½ teaspoon sugar or to taste
    ¼ teaspoon black pepper

Combine tomatoes, green onions, garlic, chili pepper, oil and lime juice in a medium bowl. Stir in cilantro, if desired. Season with salt, sugar and black pepper. Adjust seasonings to taste, adding lime juice or chili pepper, if desired. Makes about 2 cups.

Guadalajara Beef and Salsa

Tempting POULTRY

CHICKEN RIBBONS SATAY

½ cup creamy peanut butter
½ cup water
¼ cup soy sauce
4 cloves garlic, pressed
3 tablespoons lemon juice
2 tablespoons firmly packed brown sugar
¾ teaspoon ground ginger
½ teaspoon crushed red pepper flakes
4 boneless skinless chicken breast halves
Sliced green onion tops for garnish

Combine peanut butter, water, soy sauce, garlic, lemon juice, brown sugar, ginger and red pepper flakes in small saucepan. Cook over medium heat 1 minute or until smooth; cool. Remove garlic from sauce; discard. Reserve half of sauce for dipping. Cut chicken lengthwise into 1-inch-wide strips. Thread onto 8 metal or bamboo skewers. (Soak bamboo skewers in water at least 20 minutes to keep them from burning.)

Oil hot grid to help prevent sticking. Grill chicken, on a covered grill, over medium-hot Kingsford briquets, 6 to 8 minutes until chicken is cooked through, turning once. Baste with sauce once or twice during cooking. Serve with reserved sauce garnished with sliced green onion tops.

Makes 4 servings

Chicken Ribbons Satay

TURKEY GRILLING POINTERS

- Some larger turkey cuts have an automatic cooking device that pops up when the turkey is done. To determine doneness, rely on the automatic cooking device and a meat thermometer inserted in the thickest portion of turkey meat. Breast meat is done at 170°F; dark meat is done at 180°F.

- When turkey is done, the meat just under the skin may look pink. This is not a sign of undercooked meat; this is caused by the smoke from the coals.

Turkey Grilled with K.C. Masterpiece Barbecue Sauce

Turkey Product	Method	Approximate Grilling Time on Covered Grill	Brush Barbecue Sauce on During the Last Minutes of Cooking
Bone-in Turkey Breast Half 2 to 3 pounds	Indirect Heat	1 to 1½ hours	20 minutes
Bone-in Turkey Breast 4 to 6 pounds	Indirect Heat	2 to 2½ hours	20 minutes
Boneless Turkey Roast 3 pounds	Indirect Heat	1 to 1½ hours	20 minutes
Turkey Drumsticks ½ pound each	Indirect Heat	50 to 60 minutes	15 minutes
Bone-in Turkey Thighs ¾ to 1 pound each	Indirect Heat	50 minutes to 1¼ hours	15 minutes
Turkey Wings ¾ pounds each	Indirect Heat	50 to 60 minutes	15 minutes
Ground Turkey Burger ½ inch thick, ¼ pound	Direct Heat	5 to 8 minutes	3 to 4 minutes
Turkey Franks up to 2 ounces each	Direct Heat	4 to 5 minutes	2 to 3 minutes

- Warm extra K.C. Masterpiece Barbecue Sauce to serve on the side with grilled turkey.

LEMON HERBED CHICKEN

   ½ cup butter or margarine
   ½ cup vegetable oil
   ⅓ cup lemon juice
   2 tablespoons finely chopped parsley
   2 tablespoons garlic salt
   1 teaspoon dried rosemary, crushed
   1 teaspoon dried summer savory, crushed
   ½ teaspoon dried thyme, crushed
   ¼ teaspoon coarsely cracked black pepper
   6 chicken quarters (breast-wing or thigh-drumstick
      combinations)

Combine butter, oil, lemon juice, parsley, garlic salt, rosemary, summer savory, thyme and pepper in a small saucepan. Heat until butter melts. Place chicken in a shallow glass dish. Brush with some of the sauce. Let stand 10 to 15 minutes.

Oil hot grid to help prevent sticking. Place dark meat pieces on grill 10 minutes before white meat pieces (dark meat takes longer to cook). Grill chicken, on an uncovered grill, over medium-hot Kingsford briquets, 30 to 45 minutes for breast quarters or 50 to 60 minutes for leg quarters. Chicken is done when meat is no longer pink by bone. Turn quarters over and baste with sauce every 10 minutes. *Makes 6 servings*

BARBECUED TURKEY WITH HERBS

   1 turkey (9 to 13 pounds), thawed if frozen
   ¾ cup vegetable oil
   ½ cup chopped fresh parsley
   2 tablespoons chopped fresh sage *or* 2 teaspoons
      dried sage, crushed
   2 tablespoons chopped fresh rosemary *or*
      2 teaspoons dried rosemary, crushed
   1 tablespoon chopped fresh thyme *or* 1 teaspoon
      dried thyme, crushed
   Salt and cracked black pepper

Remove neck and giblets from turkey. Rinse turkey; pat dry with paper towels. Combine oil, parsley, sage, rosemary, thyme, salt and pepper in a small bowl. Brush cavities and outer surface of turkey generously with herb mixture. Pull skin over neck and secure with skewer. Tuck wings under back and tie legs together with cotton string. Insert a meat thermometer into center of thickest part of thigh, not touching bone.

Arrange medium-hot Kingsford briquets on each side of a large rectangular metal or foil drip pan. Pour in hot tap water to fill pan half full. Place turkey breast side up on grid, directly above the drip pan. Grill turkey, on a covered grill, 9 to 13 minutes per pound or until meat thermometer registers 185°F. Baste occasionally with herb mixture. Add a few briquets to both sides of the fire every hour, or as necessary, to maintain a constant temperature. Garnish with additional fresh herbs, if desired. *Makes 8 to 10 servings*

CITRUS MARINATED CHICKEN

1 cup orange juice
¼ cup lemon juice
¼ cup lime juice
2 cloves garlic, pressed or minced
4 boneless skinless chicken breast halves
Salt and black pepper
Citrus Tarragon Butter (recipe follows)
Hot cooked couscous with green onion slices and
slivered almonds (optional)
Lemon and lime slices and Italian parsley for
garnish

Combine orange, lemon and lime juices and garlic in a shallow glass dish or large heavy plastic bag. Add chicken; cover dish or close bag. Marinate in refrigerator no more than 2 hours. (Lemon and lime juice will "cook" the chicken if it's left in too long.) Remove chicken from marinade; discard marinade. Season chicken with salt and pepper.

Oil hot grid to help prevent sticking. Grill chicken, on a covered grill, over medium Kingsford briquets, 6 to 8 minutes until chicken is cooked through, turning once. Serve topped with a dollop of Citrus Tarragon Butter. Serve over couscous. Garnish, if desired. *Makes 4 servings*

CITRUS TARRAGON BUTTER

½ cup butter, softened
1 teaspoon finely grated orange peel
1 teaspoon finely grated lemon peel
1 tablespoon lemon juice
1 tablespoon orange juice
1 tablespoon finely chopped fresh tarragon

Beat butter in a small bowl until soft and light. Stir in remaining ingredients. Cover and refrigerate until ready to serve. Makes about ½ cup.

GRILLED GAME HENS

½ cup K.C. Masterpiece Barbecue Sauce
¼ cup dry sherry
3 tablespoons frozen orange juice concentrate, thawed
4 Cornish game hens (each about 1 to 1½ pounds)

Combine barbecue sauce, sherry and orange juice concentrate in a small saucepan. Bring to a boil. Simmer 10 minutes; cool. Rinse hens; pat dry with paper towels. Brush sauce onto hens. Oil hot grid to help prevent sticking. Grill hens, on a covered grill, over medium-hot Kingsford briquets, 40 to 50 minutes or until thigh moves easily and juices run clear, turning once. Baste with sauce during last 10 minutes of grilling. Remove hens from grill; baste with sauce. *Makes 4 to 6 servings*

Citrus Marinated Chicken topped with
Citrus Tarragon Butter

TURKEY PICATTA ON GRILLED ROLLS

¼ cup lemon juice
¼ cup olive oil
2 tablespoons capers in liquid, chopped
2 cloves garlic, crushed
   Black pepper to taste
1 pound turkey breast slices
4 soft French rolls, cut lengthwise into halves
4 thin slices mozzarella or Swiss cheese (optional)
   Lettuce (optional)
   Red pepper slivers (optional)
   Additional capers (optional)

Combine lemon juice, oil, 2 tablespoons capers with liquid, garlic and pepper in a shallow glass dish or large heavy plastic bag. Add turkey; cover dish or close bag. Marinate in refrigerator several hours or overnight. Remove turkey from marinade; discard marinade.

Oil hot grid to help prevent sticking. Grill turkey, on an uncovered grill, over medium-hot Kingsford briquets, 2 minutes until turkey is cooked through, turning once. Move cooked turkey slices to edge of grill to keep warm. Grill rolls, cut side down, until toasted. Fill rolls with hot turkey slices, dividing equally. Add mozzarella to sandwiches, if desired. Serve with lettuce, red pepper and additional capers, if desired.

Makes 4 servings

ORANGE–DIJON CHICKEN

Many supermarkets now carry boneless skinless chicken thighs, and they cook in even less time than boneless breasts. If you prefer dark meat, this recipe is for you.

⅓ cup vegetable oil
⅓ cup soy sauce
⅓ cup firmly packed brown sugar
⅓ cup frozen orange juice concentrate, thawed
⅓ cup Dijon mustard
8 boneless skinless chicken thighs or 8 bone-in
   skinless thighs
   Salt and black pepper

Whisk together oil, soy sauce, brown sugar, orange juice concentrate and mustard in medium bowl. Place chicken in a shallow glass dish or large heavy plastic bag. Pour marinade over chicken; cover dish or close bag. Marinate in refrigerator at least 2 hours, turning several times. Remove chicken from marinade; discard marinade. Season chicken with salt and pepper.

Oil hot grid to help prevent sticking. Grill chicken, on a covered grill, over medium Kingsford briquets, 4 to 7 minutes for boneless thighs and 15 minutes for bone-in thighs, turning once or twice. Chicken is done when meat is no longer pink in center.

Makes 4 servings

Turkey Picatta on Grilled Rolls

GRILLED TURKEY BREAST WITH FRUIT VINAIGRETTE

Leftovers make delicious sandwiches. Try our sandwich spreads on page 91.

¾ cup orange juice
½ cup walnut or hazelnut oil*
½ cup vegetable oil*
¼ cup raspberry, blueberry or apple cider vinegar
1 tablespoon sugar
1 teaspoon salt
1 teaspoon black pepper
1 boneless turkey breast (1½ to 2 pounds)

Whisk together orange juice, both oils, vinegar, sugar, salt and pepper in medium bowl. Reserve half of the vinaigrette. Place turkey in a shallow glass dish or large heavy plastic bag. Pour remaining vinaigrette over turkey; cover dish or close bag. Marinate in refrigerator up to 12 hours, turning once or twice. Remove turkey from marinade; discard marinade.

Arrange medium-hot Kingsford briquets on both sides of a metal or foil drip pan. Pour in hot tap water to fill pan half full. Oil hot grid to help prevent sticking. Grill turkey, on a covered grill, 25 to 30 minutes per pound until a meat thermometer inserted in the thickest part registers 170°F. Let turkey stand 10 minutes before slicing. Slice and serve with reserved vinaigrette. *Makes 6 servings*

*Substitute 1 cup light olive oil or avocado oil for the nut oil and vegetable oil.

GRILLED CURRY CHICKEN WITH COCONUT RICE

4 large chicken legs (thigh-drumstick combination)
  Salt and ground black pepper
2 tablespoons curry powder
2 tablespoons chili powder
2 tablespoons vegetable oil
  Coconut Rice (page 45)

Season chicken generously with salt and pepper. Combine curry powder, chili powder and oil in small bowl until mixture forms a paste. Rub paste onto chicken.

Arrange medium Kingsford briquets on each side of a rectangular metal or foil drip pan. Pour in hot tap water to fill pan half full. Oil hot grid to help prevent sticking. Place chicken on grid directly above drip pan. Grill chicken, on a covered grill, 50 to 60 minutes, until a meat thermometer inserted into the thickest part registers 180°F. Chicken is done when meat is no longer pink by bone. Serve with Coconut Rice. *Makes 4 servings*

continued on page 45

COCONUT RICE

1 cup Basmati* or other long-grain white rice
Chicken broth
Canned coconut milk

Prepare rice according to package directions *except* omit salt and butter or oil and substitute chicken broth for half of water and coconut milk for the other half of water.

*Basmati is a long-grain rice with a fine texture and a nutty aroma and flavor. It is available in large supermarkets and Indian markets.

TANDOORI TURKEY KABOBS

A "tandoor" is a traditional Indian large clay oven fueled by wood or charcoal which quickly sears foods, sealing in juices. Your barbecue grill can do the same. Serve with raita, a traditional East Indian yogurt sauce.

1 teaspoon ground cumin
½ teaspoon salt
¼ teaspoon ground red pepper
¼ teaspoon ground cinnamon
¼ teaspoon ground cloves
2 small cloves garlic, minced
1 tablespoon finely minced or grated fresh ginger
1 small jalapeño chili pepper, seeded and minced (optional)
1 turkey breast tenderloin (about 1 to 1¼ pounds), cut into ¾-inch cubes
1 to 2 tablespoons vegetable oil
Raita (recipe follows)
4 pita breads, cut into halves (optional)

Combine cumin, salt, red pepper, cinnamon and cloves in a small bowl; set aside ½ teaspoon spice mixture for the raita. To the remaining spice mixture add garlic, ginger and chili pepper. Place turkey in a large bowl; drizzle oil over turkey and toss lightly to coat. Sprinkle on spice mixture and again toss to coat evenly. Thread turkey onto metal or bamboo skewers. (Soak bamboo skewers in water at least 20 minutes to keep them from burning.)

Oil hot grid to help prevent sticking. Grill turkey, on a covered grill, over medium-hot Kingsford briquets, 7 to 12 minutes until turkey is cooked through, turning once. Serve with Raita and pita breads to make sandwiches, if desired.   *Makes 4 servings*

RAITA

1 cup plain low-fat yogurt
¾ cup finely diced seeded peeled cucumber
1½ tablespoons finely chopped fresh mint
2 to 3 teaspoons honey

Combine all ingredients *plus* the reserved ½ teaspoon spice mixture from the Tandoori Turkey Kabobs in a small bowl. Cover and refrigerate until ready to serve. Makes about 1½ cups.

HOT, SPICY, TANGY, STICKY CHICKEN

1 chicken (3½ to 4 pounds), cut up
1 cup cider vinegar
1 tablespoon Worcestershire sauce
1 tablespoon chili powder
1 teaspoon salt
1 teaspoon black pepper
1 teaspoon hot pepper sauce
¾ cup K.C. Masterpiece Barbecue Sauce (about)

Place chicken in a shallow glass dish or large heavy plastic bag. Combine vinegar, Worcestershire sauce, chili powder, salt, pepper and hot pepper sauce in small bowl; pour over chicken pieces. Cover dish or close bag. Marinate in refrigerator at least 4 hours, turning several times.

Oil hot grid to help prevent sticking. Place dark meat pieces on grill 10 minutes before white meat pieces (dark meat takes longer to cook). Grill chicken, on a covered grill, over medium Kingsford briquets, 30 to 45 minutes, turning once or twice. Turn and baste with K.C. Masterpiece Barbecue Sauce the last 10 minutes of cooking. Remove chicken from grill; baste with sauce. Chicken is done when meat is no longer pink by bone.

Makes 4 servings

BARBECUED TURKEY BREAST

1 bone-in turkey breast (about 5 pounds)
¼ cup firmly packed dark brown sugar
2 tablespoons paprika
1 tablespoon minced garlic
1 teaspoon salt
1 teaspoon black pepper
½ teaspoon ground red pepper
1½ cups K.C. Masterpiece Barbecue Sauce (about)

Rinse turkey; pat dry with paper towels. Combine brown sugar, paprika, garlic, salt and peppers in small bowl; rub sugar mixture on inside and outside of turkey breast.

Arrange medium Kingsford briquets on each side of a rectangular metal or foil drip pan. Pour in hot tap water to fill pan half full. Oil hot grid to help prevent sticking. Place turkey breast on grid directly above drip pan. Grill turkey, on a covered grill, 20 to 24 minutes per pound until a meat thermometer inserted in the thickest part registers 170°F. If your grill has a thermometer, maintain a cooking temperature of about 300°F. Add a few more briquets to both sides of the fire after 45 minutes to 1 hour, or as necessary, to maintain a constant temperature. Warm about 1 cup barbecue sauce in a small saucepan to serve with turkey. Brush remaining ½ cup sauce on turkey during the last 20 to 30 minutes of cooking. Let turkey stand 10 minutes before slicing.

Makes 6 to 8 servings

Hot, Spicy, Tangy, Sticky Chicken

CHICKEN WITH MEDITERRANEAN SALSA

¼ cup olive oil
3 tablespoons lemon juice
4 to 6 boneless skinless chicken breast halves
Salt and black pepper
Rosemary sprigs (optional)
Mediterranean Salsa (recipe follows)
Additional rosemary sprigs for garnish

Combine olive oil and lemon juice in a shallow glass dish; add chicken. Turn breasts to lightly coat with mixture; let stand 10 to 15 minutes. Remove chicken from dish and wipe off excess oil; season with salt and pepper.

Oil hot grid to help prevent sticking. Place chicken on grid and place a sprig of rosemary on each breast. Grill chicken, on a covered grill, over medium Kingsford briquets, 10 to 15 minutes until chicken is cooked through, turning once or twice. Serve with Mediterranean Salsa. Garnish, if desired.

Makes 4 to 6 servings

MEDITERRANEAN SALSA

2 tablespoons olive oil
2 tablespoons white wine vinegar
1 clove garlic, minced
2 tablespoons finely chopped fresh basil *or*
    1 teaspoon dried basil leaves, crushed
1 tablespoon finely chopped fresh rosemary *or*
    1 teaspoon dried rosemary, crushed
1 teaspoon sugar
¼ teaspoon black pepper
10 to 15 kalamata olives*, seeded and coarsely
    chopped *or* ⅓ cup coarsely chopped whole
    pitted ripe olives
½ cup chopped seeded cucumber
¼ cup finely chopped red onion
1 cup chopped seeded tomatoes (about ½ pound)
⅓ cup crumbled feta cheese

Combine oil, vinegar, garlic, basil, rosemary, sugar and pepper in a medium bowl. Add olives, cucumber and onion; toss to coat. Cover and refrigerate until ready to serve. Just before serving, gently stir in tomatoes and feta cheese. Makes about 2 cups.

*Kalamata olives are brine-cured Greek-style olives. They are available in large supermarkets.

Chicken with Mediterranean Salsa

GRILLED CHICKEN BREAST
WITH GAZPACHO SALSA

Low in calories but high in flavor.

  1 cup finely diced seeded tomato
  ½ cup finely diced seeded cucumber
  ½ cup finely diced green bell pepper
  ¼ cup finely chopped red or green onion
  2 tablespoons olive oil
  1 clove garlic, minced
  1 tablespoon red wine vinegar
  1 tablespoon finely chopped fresh cilantro
  1 tablespoon finely chopped fresh mint
  ¾ teaspoon salt
  ¼ teaspoon ground cumin
  ¼ teaspoon hot pepper sauce
  6 boneless skinless chicken breast halves
    Additional salt
    Black pepper
    Cilantro for garnish

To make Gazpacho Salsa, combine tomato, cucumber, green pepper, onion, oil, garlic, vinegar, cilantro, mint, salt, cumin and hot pepper sauce in a small bowl; adjust flavors to taste. Season chicken with additional salt and pepper.

Oil grid to help prevent sticking. Grill chicken, on a covered grill, over medium Kingsford briquets, 6 to 8 minutes until chicken is cooked through, turning once. Top grilled chicken with Gazpacho Salsa. Garnish with cilantro sprigs. *Makes 6 servings*

MICRO-GRILLED TURKEY
BREAST

  1 turkey breast half (about 3 pounds)
  2 tablespoons vegetable oil
  2 tablespoons lemon juice
  2 cloves garlic, pressed
  2 teaspoons chili powder
  1 teaspoon dried oregano leaves, crushed
    Salt and black pepper to taste

Rinse turkey; pat dry with paper towels. Combine oil, lemon juice, garlic, chili powder, oregano, salt and pepper in a small bowl. Brush lemon mixture over turkey breast. Place turkey in microwave-safe baking dish; cover loosely with plastic wrap. Microwave on MEDIUM (50% power) 12 to 15 minutes per pound until a meat thermometer inserted into thickest portion of breast registers 165°F.*

Oil hot grid to help prevent sticking. Grill turkey, on a covered grill, over medium Kingsford briquets, 10 minutes until skin is crisp and browned, turning once. *Makes 6 servings*

*This recipe was tested in a 700-watt microwave oven. If your oven's wattage is different, the cooking time will need to be adjusted.

CHICKEN CARIBBEAN

½ cup frozen pineapple juice concentrate, thawed
⅓ cup lime juice
¼ cup firmly packed brown sugar
¼ cup soy sauce
¼ cup water
¼ cup molasses
¼ teaspoon ground red pepper
6 boneless skinless chicken breast halves
Salt

Combine pineapple juice concentrate, lime juice, brown sugar, soy sauce, water, molasses and ground red pepper in a shallow glass dish or large heavy plastic bag until sugar is dissolved. Add chicken; cover dish or close bag. Marinate in refrigerator up to 6 hours, turning once. Remove chicken from marinade; pour marinade into a saucepan. Cook marinade at a low boil until reduced to about ½ cup and it has a syruplike consistency, stirring often. Season chicken with salt.

Oil hot grid to help prevent sticking. Grill chicken, on a covered grill, over medium Kingsford briquets, 10 to 15 minutes until chicken is cooked through, turning one or twice. Baste with glaze 3 or 4 times during cooking.

Makes 6 servings

GRILLED TURKEY STEAKS

½ cup frozen pineapple juice concentrate, thawed
3 tablespoons seasoned rice vinegar
½ cup soy sauce
½ cup water
⅓ cup firmly packed brown sugar
1 tablespoon finely grated fresh ginger
1 tablespoon pressed or minced garlic
½ to 1 teaspoon crushed red pepper flakes (optional)
1 boneless skinless turkey half breast
(1½ to 2 pounds), cut into 1-inch-thick slices
1 tablespoon cornstarch
Salt
Vegetable oil

Combine first 8 ingredients in a medium bowl. Reserve 1 cup of marinade. Place turkey in a shallow glass dish or large heavy plastic bag. Pour remaining marinade over turkey; cover dish or close bag. Marinate in refrigerator at least 2 hours, turning several times. Place reserved marinade in 2-cup glass measuring cup; whisk in cornstarch. Microwave on HIGH (100% power) 2 minutes. Stir; microwave on HIGH 30 to 60 seconds longer until thickened to a glaze; set aside.* Remove turkey from marinade; discard marinade. Season lightly with salt. Brush lightly with oil.

Oil hot grid to help prevent sticking. Grill turkey, on a covered grill, over medium Kingsford briquets, 5 to 8 minutes until turkey is cooked through, turning several times and brushing with glaze the last 1 or 2 minutes of cooking.

Makes 4 to 6 servings

*This recipe was tested in a 700-watt microwave oven. If your oven's wattage is different, the cooking time will need to be adjusted.

LEMON-GARLIC ROASTED CHICKEN

The chicken is delicious served simply with its own juices, but this garlic sauce is so good you may want to double the recipe.

1 chicken (3½ to 4 pounds)
Salt and black pepper
2 tablespoons butter or margarine, softened
2 lemons, cut into halves
4 to 6 cloves garlic, peeled, left whole
5 to 6 sprigs fresh rosemary
Garlic Sauce (recipe follows)
Additional rosemary sprigs and lemon wedges for garnish

Rinse chicken; pat dry with paper towels. Season with salt and pepper, then rub the skin with butter. Place lemons, garlic and rosemary in cavity of chicken. Tuck wings under back and tie legs together with cotton string.

Arrange medium-low Kingsford briquets on each side of a rectangular metal or foil drip pan. Pour in hot tap water to fill pan half full. Place chicken breast side up on grid, directly above the drip pan. Grill chicken, on a covered grill, about 1 hour until a meat thermometer inserted in the thigh registers 175° to 180°F or until the joints move easily and juices run clear when chicken is pierced. Add a few briquets to both sides of the fire, if necessary, to maintain a constant temperature.

While the chicken is cooking, prepare Garlic Sauce. When chicken is done, carefully lift it from the grill to a wide shallow bowl so that all the juices from the cavity run into the bowl. Transfer juices to a small bowl or gravy boat. Carve chicken; serve with Garlic Sauce and cooking juices. Garnish with additional rosemary sprigs and lemon wedges.   *Makes 4 servings*

GARLIC SAUCE

2 tablespoons olive oil
1 large head of garlic, cloves separated and peeled
2 (1-inch-wide) strips lemon peel
1 can (14½ ounces) low-salt chicken broth
½ cup water
1 sprig *each* sage and oregano *or* 2 to 3 sprigs parsley
¼ cup butter, softened

Heat oil in a saucepan; add garlic cloves and lemon peel; sauté over medium-low heat, stirring frequently, until garlic just starts to brown in a few spots. Add broth, water and herbs; simmer to reduce mixture by about half. Discard herb sprigs and lemon peel. Transfer broth mixture to blender or food processor; process until smooth. Return garlic purée to the saucepan and whisk in butter over very low heat until smooth. Sauce can be rewarmed before serving. Makes about 1 cup.

Lemon-Garlic Roasted Chicken

TURKEY BURRITOS

This recipe is great for casual get-togethers. Just prepare the fixings and let the guests make their own burritos.

1 tablespoon ground cumin
1 tablespoon chili powder
1½ teaspoons salt
1½ to 2 pounds turkey tenderloin, cut into ½-inch
    cubes
Avocado-Corn Salsa (recipe follows)
Lime wedges
Flour tortillas
Sour cream (optional)
Tomato slices for garnish

Combine cumin, chili powder and salt in cup. Place turkey cubes in a shallow glass dish or large heavy plastic bag; pour dry rub over turkey and thoroughly coat. Let turkey stand while preparing Avocado-Corn Salsa. Thread turkey on metal or bamboo skewers. (Soak bamboo skewers in water at least 20 minutes to prevent them from burning).

Oil hot grid to help prevent sticking. Grill turkey, on a covered grill, over medium Kingsford briquets, about 6 minutes until turkey is cooked through, turning once. Remove skewers from grill; squeeze lime wedges on skewers. Warm flour tortillas in the microwave oven, or brush each tortilla very lightly with water and grill 10 to 15 seconds per side. Top with Avocado-Corn Salsa and sour cream, if desired. Garnish with tomato slices.

Makes 6 servings

AVOCADO-CORN SALSA

2 small to medium, ripe avocados, finely diced
1 cup cooked fresh corn or thawed frozen corn
2 medium tomatoes, seeded, finely diced
2 to 3 tablespoons lime juice
2 to 3 tablespoons chopped fresh cilantro
½ to 1 teaspoon minced hot green chili pepper
½ teaspoon salt

Gently stir together all ingredients in a medium bowl; adjust flavors to taste. Cover and refrigerate until ready to serve. Makes about 1½ cups.

Turkey Burritos and Avocado-Corn Salsa

GRILLED CHICKEN WITH ASIAN PESTO

Boneless skinless poultry parts are convenient for after work grilling because they cook so quickly.

4 boneless skinless chicken breast halves *or*
    8 boneless skinless thighs *or* a combination of
    both
    Olive or vegetable oil
    Salt and black pepper
    Asian Pesto (recipe follows)
    Lime wedges

Place chicken between two pieces of waxed paper; pound to ⅜-inch thickness. Brush chicken with oil; season with salt and pepper. Spread about ½ tablespoon Asian Pesto on both sides of each breast or thigh.

Oil hot grid to help prevent sticking. Grill chicken, on an uncovered grill, over medium Kingsford briquets, 6 to 8 minutes until chicken is cooked through, turning once. Serve with additional Asian Pesto and lime wedges.

Makes 4 servings

ASIAN PESTO

    1 cup packed fresh basil
    1 cup packed fresh cilantro
    1 cup packed fresh mint leaves
    ¼ cup olive or vegetable oil
    2 cloves garlic, chopped
    2½ to 3½ tablespoons lime juice
    1 tablespoon sugar
    1 teaspoon salt
    1 teaspoon black pepper

Combine all ingredients in a blender or food processor; process to a smooth paste. Makes about ¾ cup.

Note: The Asian Pesto recipe makes enough for 6 servings. Leftovers can be saved and used as a spread for sandwiches.

TURKEY SKEWERS WITH CRANBERRY–GINGER SAUCE

    1 medium orange
    ⅓ cup soy sauce
    2 tablespoons water
    1 tablespoon minced fresh ginger
    2 turkey breast tenderloins (1¼ to 1¾ pounds total),
        cut into ¾-inch cubes
    Salt and black pepper
    Cranberry-Ginger Sauce (page 57)

continued on page 57

Juice orange and coarsely chop up remaining fruit, including rind. Combine juice, chopped orange, soy sauce, water and ginger in a shallow glass dish or large heavy plastic bag. Add turkey; cover dish or close bag. Marinate in refrigerator up to 4 hours, turning once or twice. Remove turkey from marinade; discard marinade. Thread turkey on metal or bamboo skewers. (Soak bamboo skewers in water at least 20 minutes to keep them from burning.) Season lightly with salt and pepper.

Oil hot grid to help prevent sticking. Grill turkey, on a covered grill, over medium Kingsford briquets, 7 to 12 minutes until turkey is cooked through, turning once. Serve with Cranberry-Ginger Sauce.   *Makes 4 to 6 servings*

CRANBERRY–GINGER SAUCE

2 cans (16 ounces each) whole-berry cranberry
   sauce
1½ teaspoons finely grated orange peel
1½ tablespoons minced fresh ginger
¼ cup orange juice

Combine all ingredients in a saucepan; simmer gently about 10 minutes. Serve warm with turkey skewers. Makes about 4 cups.

HERB MARINATED CHICKEN

1 chicken (3½ to 4 pounds), cut up
¼ cup water
3 tablespoons red wine vinegar
2 tablespoons Dijon mustard
1 large clove garlic, minced
1 teaspoon salt
1 teaspoon black pepper
1 teaspoon sugar
1 tablespoon finely chopped fresh rosemary *or*
   ¾ teaspoon dried rosemary leaves, crushed
1 tablespoon finely chopped fresh thyme *or*
   ¾ teaspoon dried thyme leaves, crushed
1 tablespoon finely chopped fresh tarragon *or*
   ¾ teaspoon dried tarragon leaves, crushed
½ cup olive oil

Place chicken in a shallow glass dish or large heavy plastic bag. Whisk together water, vinegar, mustard, garlic, salt, pepper, sugar, rosemary, thyme and tarragon in small bowl; continue whisking while slowly adding olive oil. Pour mixture over chicken; cover dish or close bag. Marinate in refrigerator at least 4 hours, turning once or twice. Remove chicken from marinade; discard marinade.

Oil hot grid to help prevent sticking. Place dark meat pieces on grill 10 minutes before white meat pieces (dark meat takes longer to cook). Grill chicken, on a covered grill, over medium Kingsford briquets, 30 to 45 minutes, turning once or twice. Chicken is done when meat is no longer pink by bone.   *Makes 4 servings*

CHICKEN CAESAR

¾ cup olive oil
¼ cup lemon juice
¼ cup finely grated Parmesan cheese
1 can (2 ounces) anchovies, drained and chopped
1 clove garlic, minced
2 teaspoons Dijon mustard
½ teaspoon black pepper
   Salt
4 boneless skinless chicken breast halves
½ pound green beans, trimmed, cooked and cooled
6 to 8 small new potatoes, cooked, cooled and cut
      into quarters
¾ cup cooked fresh corn or thawed frozen corn
1 medium carrot, thinly sliced
10 to 12 cherry tomatoes, cut into halves
2 green onions, sliced
   Finely chopped parsley or basil

To make Caesar Dressing, place first 7 ingredients in blender or food processor; process until smooth and creamy. Add salt to taste.

Place chicken in a shallow glass dish. Pour ¼ cup dressing over chicken; turn to coat. Let stand while preparing vegetables, or cover and refrigerate up to 4 hours. Place vegetables in a large bowl; toss with remaining dressing; spoon onto serving plates. Season lightly with salt.

Oil hot grid to help prevent sticking, Grill chicken, on a covered grill, over medium Kingsford briquets, 6 to 8 minutes until chicken is cooked through, turning once. Slice chicken crosswise and serve with vegetables. Sprinkle on parsley or basil. Serve immediately or at room temperature.

Makes 4 servings

MICRO–GRILLED CHICKEN

¼ cup soy sauce
2 tablespoons firmly packed brown sugar
2 cloves garlic, pressed
½ teaspoon dry mustard
½ teaspoon paprika
1 chicken (about 3 pounds), cut up

Combine first 5 ingredients in a small bowl. Arrange chicken in a single layer in 13×9-inch microwave-safe baking dish; place meatiest portions to outside edge. Pour soy mixture over chicken; turn to coat. Cover loosely with plastic wrap. Microwave on HIGH (100% power) 15 to 18 minutes, rearranging pieces halfway through cooking.* Chicken is done when juices run clear.

Oil hot grid to help prevent sticking. Grill chicken, on a covered grill, over medium Kingsford briquets, 10 minutes until skin is crisp and browned, turning once.   *Makes 4 to 6 servings*

*This recipe was tested in a 700-watt microwave oven. If your oven's wattage is different, the cooking time will need to be adjusted.

Chicken Caesar

Quick & Fabulous
SEAFOOD

SNAPPER WITH PESTO BUTTER

½ cup butter or margarine, softened
1 cup packed fresh basil leaves, coarsely chopped *or*
    ½ cup chopped fresh parsley *plus* 2
    tablespoons dried basil leaves, chopped
3 tablespoons finely grated fresh Parmesan cheese
1 clove garlic, minced
    Olive oil
2 to 3 teaspoons lemon juice
4 to 6 red snapper, rock cod, salmon or other
    medium-firm fish fillets (at least ½ inch thick)
    Salt and black pepper
    Lemon wedges
    Fresh basil or parsley sprigs and lemon strips for
    garnish

To make Pesto Butter, place butter, basil, cheese, garlic and 1 tablespoon oil in blender or food processor; process until blended. Add lemon juice to taste. Rinse fish; pat dry with paper towels. Brush one side of fish lightly with oil; season with salt and pepper.

Oil hot grid to help prevent sticking. Grill fillets oil side down, on a covered grill, over medium Kingsford briquets, 5 to 9 minutes. Halfway through cooking time, brush top with oil and season with salt and pepper, then turn and continue grilling until fish turns from translucent to opaque throughout. (Grilling time depends on the thickness of fish; allow 3 to 5 minutes for each ½ inch of thickness.) Serve each fillet with a spoonful of Pesto Butter and a wedge of lemon. Garnish with basil sprigs and lemon strips. *Makes 4 to 6 servings*

Snapper with Pesto Butter

POINTERS FOR GRILLING FISH

- Firm-textured fish, such as swordfish, shark, tuna New Zealand hoki and monkfish, are excellent choices for grilling because they don't fall apart easily when grilled.

- Medium-firm fish, such as salmon, mahi-mahi, grouper, orange roughy, halibut and cod, are well suited for grilling, too. These fish are easiest to handle as steaks, fillets with the skin on or fillets at least ¾ inch thick.

- Fish high in oil, such as salmon, bluefish and mackerel, are good for the grill because they retain their moisture in the high, dry heat of grilling and because their flavors are enhanced by smoke.

- Delicate fish, such as sole, flounder, sand dabs or sable fish, are generally less suitable for grilling. They tend to fall through the grid and their delicate flavor is overwhelmed by the smoke.

- Purchase steak and fillets that are at least ½ inch thick; anything thinner will quickly overcook and easily fall apart on the grid.

- To prevent sticking, the grid should be very clean. Heat the grid 2 or 3 minutes over hot coals, then brush lightly with oil. Baste fish prior to turning to keep it from sticking to the grid.

- Allow 3 to 5 minutes cooking time for each ½ inch of thickness. Fish continues to cook off the grill and you can always return it to cook a bit longer if necessary.

- To test for doneness separate the fish with a fork or tip of a knife. The flesh will be just slightly translucent in the center, and it will look very moist. As you remove it from the grill the fish will turn from translucent to opaque throughout.

- Using a grill cover will intensify the smoky flavor and help keep fish moist and tender.

- If you marinate fish, 15 to 30 minutes is all the time you'll need. Long immersion in high-acid marinades (lemon juice, wine, vinegar) causes fish to "cook"—like seviche—it actually turns opaque and firm.

- To thread shrimp on a skewer, pierce both the "shoulder" and tail so shrimp forms a U on the skewer.

COMPOUND BUTTERS FOR GRILLED FISH OR CHICKEN

• *Keep these on hand for mid-week grilling!*

• *Compound butters are a quick and easy way to flavor grilled fish and poultry. They can be made ahead, shaped in a roll and refrigerated or frozen. Slice off what you need and place it on the hot food immediately after removing from the grill. The Honey-Lime Butter can also be melted and used for basting.*

• *Once blended, shape butter into a roll about 1 inch in diameter. Wrap in plastic wrap. Refrigerate up to 1 week; freeze up to 6 weeks.*

MELON BUTTER

> 1 cup coarsely chopped cantaloupe, papaya or
>   peaches
> ½ cup butter or margarine, softened
> 2 tablespoons lime juice
> 1 teaspoon finely grated lime peel
> ¼ teaspoon black pepper

In a small saucepan, simmer fruit until softened or microwave fruit in a small microwave-safe dish on HIGH (100% power) 3 minutes.* Cool to room temperature. Place all ingredients in a blender or food processor; process until smooth. Makes about ⅔ cup.

*This recipe was tested in a 700-watt microwave oven. If your oven's wattage is different, the cooking time will need to be adjusted.

HONEY–LIME BUTTER

> ½ cup butter or margarine, softened
> 3 to 4 tablespoons lime juice
> 1 tablespoon honey
> 1 clove garlic, pressed or minced
> 1 teaspoon finely grated lime peel
> ¼ to ½ teaspoon crushed red pepper flakes

Beat all ingredients in a small bowl until well blended. Makes about ¾ cup.

Variation: Add minced or grated ginger.

NIÇOISE BUTTER

> ½ cup butter or margarine, softened
> ¼ cup niçoise olives, pitted, finely chopped
> 2 tablespoons finely chopped fresh basil

Beat all ingredients in a small bowl until well blended. Makes about ⅔ cup.

GRILLED HERB TROUT

Just-caught perch, pike or any other whole freshwater fish can be substituted for the trout. The bacon bastes and flavors the trout as it grills. Grilled with the skin on, the fish won't dry out.

> 6 whole cleaned trout (each at least 10 ounces),
>   head removed if desired, boned and butterflied
>   Salt and black pepper
> 6 slices bacon slices
> 6 sprigs dill or tarragon
> 1 or 2 medium onions, cut into wedges
>   Lemon wedges
>   Dill or tarragon sprigs for garnish
>   Grilled New Potatoes (recipe follows)

Rinse fish; pat dry with paper towels. Season lightly with salt and pepper. Place 1 slice of bacon and 1 herb sprig in the cavity of each trout; close fish. (There's no need to tie the fish; it will remain closed during cooking.) Place fish in a fish basket, if desired.

Oil hot grid to help prevent sticking. Grill fish, on a covered grill, over medium-hot Kingsford briquets, 8 to 12 minutes. Halfway through cooking time, turn fish and add onions to grill. Continue grilling until fish turns from transparent to opaque throughout. Serve with lemon. (The bacon does not become crispy; it flavors and bastes the fish during cooking. It can be removed, if desired, just before serving.) Garnish with dill.

Makes 6 servings

Grilled New Potatoes: Cook or microwave new potatoes until barely tender. Cut into halves. Brush lightly with oil; season with salt and pepper. Grill over medium-hot Kingsford briquets, 8 to 10 minutes, turning occasionally.

BARBECUED SALMON

> 4 salmon steaks (at least ¾ inch thick)
> 3 tablespoons lemon juice
> 2 tablespoons soy sauce
>   Salt and black pepper
> ½ cup K.C. Masterpiece Barbecue Sauce (about)

Rinse fish; pat dry with paper towels. Combine lemon juice and soy sauce in a shallow glass dish. Place steaks in dish; let stand at cool room temperature no more than 15 to 20 minutes, turning steaks several times. Remove fish; discard marinade. Season lightly with salt and pepper.

Oil hot grid to help prevent sticking. Grill salmon, on a covered grill, over medium Kingsford briquets, 10 to 14 minutes. Halfway through cooking time, brush top with barbecue sauce, then turn and continue grilling until fish turns from translucent to opaque throughout. (Grilling time depends on thickness of the fish; allow 3 to 5 minutes for each ½ inch of thickness.) Remove fish from grill; brush with barbecue sauce. *Makes 4 servings*

Grilled Herb Trout

SHRIMP SKEWERS WITH TROPICAL FRUIT SALSA

½ cup soy sauce
¼ cup lime juice
2 cloves garlic, minced
1½ pounds large shrimp, shelled and deveined
Tropical Fruit Salsa (recipe follows)
Vegetable oil
Salt and black pepper

Combine soy sauce, lime juice and garlic in a shallow glass dish or large heavy plastic bag. Add shrimp; cover dish or close bag. Marinate in refrigerator no longer than 30 minutes.

Meanwhile, prepare Tropical Fruit Salsa. (Salsa should not be made more than two hours before serving.)

Remove shrimp from marinade; discard marinade. Thread shrimp on metal or bamboo skewers. (Soak bamboo skewers in water at least 20 minutes to keep them from burning.) Brush one side of shrimp lightly with oil; season with salt and pepper.

Oil hot grid to help prevent sticking. Grill shrimp oil side down, on a covered grill, over medium-hot Kingsford briquets, 6 to 8 minutes. Halfway through cooking time, brush top with oil, season with salt and pepper, then turn and continue grilling until shrimp firm up and turn opaque throughout. Serve with Tropical Fruit Salsa.   *Makes 4 servings*

TROPICAL FRUIT SALSA

2 mangos*
2 kiwifruit
3 tablespoons finely chopped or finely slivered red
    onion
3 tablespoons lime juice
¼ teaspoon salt
¼ teaspoon crushed red pepper flakes
1 teaspoon sugar
1 tablespoon finely chopped fresh mint leaves
1 tablespoon finely chopped fresh cilantro

Peel fruit. Cut mango into ¼-inch pieces; cut kiwifruit into wedges. Combine with remaining ingredients in medium bowl; adjust flavors to taste. Cover and refrigerate no more than 2 hours. Makes about 1 cup.

*Substitute 1 papaya or 2 large or 3 medium peaches for the mangos.

Tip: Mangos are available most of the year in many large supermarkets. They are ripe when they yield to gentle pressure; the color of the skin does not indicate ripeness. Unripe mangos will ripen in a few days when stored at room temperature. The mango has a long, flat seed in the center of the fruit that adheres to the flesh. To dice the fruit, first peel the skin, then cut it lengthwise away from the seed, then cut crosswise into ¼-inch pieces.

Shrimp Skewers with Tropical Fruit Salsa

CATFISH WITH FRESH CORN RELISH

4 catfish fillets (each about 6 ounces and at least
   ½ inch thick)
2 tablespoons paprika
½ teaspoon ground red pepper
½ teaspoon salt
   Fresh Corn Relish (recipe follows)
   Lime wedges
   Grilled Baking Potatoes (optional) (page 32)
   Tarragon sprigs for garnish

Rinse fish; pat dry with paper towels. Combine paprika, red pepper and salt in cup; lightly sprinkle on both sides of fish.

Oil hot grid to help prevent sticking. Grill fish, on a covered grill, over medium Kingsford briquets, 5 to 9 minutes. Halfway through cooking time, turn fish over and continue grilling until fish turns from translucent to opaque throughout. (Grilling time depends on the thickness of fish; allow 3 to 5 minutes for each ½ inch of thickness.) Serve with Fresh Corn Relish, lime wedges and potatoes, if desired. Garnish with tarragon sprigs.

Makes 4 servings

FRESH CORN RELISH

¾ cup cooked fresh corn or thawed frozen corn
¼ cup finely diced green bell pepper
¼ cup finely slivered red onion
1 tablespoon vegetable oil
2 tablespoons seasoned (sweet) rice vinegar
   Salt and black pepper
½ cup cherry tomatoes, cut into quarters

Toss together corn, bell pepper, onion, oil and vinegar in a medium bowl. Season with salt and pepper. Cover and refrigerate until ready to serve. Just before serving, gently mix in tomatoes. Makes about 1½ cups.

Catfish with Fresh Corn Relish

SEAFOOD KABOBS

24 large sea scallops
12 medium shrimp, shelled and deveined
1 can (8½ ounces) whole small artichoke hearts, drained and cut into halves
2 red or yellow peppers, cut into 2-inch pieces
¼ cup olive or vegetable oil
¼ cup lime juice
Lime slices and sage sprigs for garnish

Thread scallops, shrimp, artichoke hearts and peppers alternately on metal or bamboo skewers. (Soak bamboo skewers in water at least 20 minutes to keep them from burning.) Combine oil and lime juice in a small bowl; brush kabobs with lime mixture.

Oil hot grid to help prevent sticking. Grill kabobs, on an uncovered grill, over low Kingsford briquets, 6 to 8 minutes. Halfway through cooking time, baste top with lime mixture, then turn kabobs and continue grilling until scallops and shrimp firm up and turn opaque throughout. Remove kabobs from grill; baste with lime mixture. Garnish with lime slices and sage sprigs.

Makes 6 servings

SWORDFISH WITH HONEY–LIME GLAZE

½ cup lime juice
3½ tablespoons honey
2 cloves garlic, minced
½ to 1 serrano or jalapeño chili pepper, fresh or canned, seeded and minced
1½ teaspoons cornstarch
Salt
2 tablespoons finely chopped fresh cilantro (optional)
6 swordfish steaks (at least ¾ inch thick)
Black pepper
2 cups diced seeded tomatoes (about 1½ pounds)
Cilantro sprigs for garnish

To make Honey-Lime Glaze, combine lime juice, honey, garlic, chili pepper, cornstarch and ½ teaspoon salt in a small saucepan. Boil about 1 minute until slightly thickened, stirring constantly. Stir in cilantro, if desired. Reserve half of Honey-Lime Glaze in a small bowl; cool. Rinse steaks; pat dry with paper towels. Season fish with salt and pepper. Brush fish with some of the remaining glaze.

Oil hot grid to help prevent sticking. Grill fish, on a covered grill, over medium Kingsford briquets, 6 to 10 minutes. Halfway through cooking time, brush top with glaze, then turn and continue grilling until fish turns from transparent to opaque throughout. (Grilling time depends on the thickness of fish; allow 3 to 5 minutes for each ½ inch of thickness.) Stir tomatoes into reserved, cooled glaze and serve as a topping for fish. Garnish with cilantro sprigs.

Makes 6 servings

Seafood Kabobs

GRILLED FISH STEAKS WITH TOMATO BASIL BUTTER SAUCE

Tomato Basil Butter Sauce (recipe follows)
4 fish steaks, such as halibut, swordfish, tuna or
    salmon (at least ¾ inch thick)
Olive oil
Salt and black pepper
Fresh basil leaves and summer squash slices for
    garnish
Hot cooked seasoned noodles (optional)

Prepare Tomato Basil Butter Sauce; set aside. Rinse fish; pat dry with paper towels. Brush one side of fish lightly with oil; season with salt and pepper.

Oil hot grid to help prevent sticking. Grill fish oil side down, on a covered grill, over medium Kingsford briquets, 6 to 10 minutes. Halfway through cooking time, brush top with oil and season with salt and pepper, then turn and continue grilling until fish turns from translucent to opaque throughout. (Grilling time depends on the thickness of fish; allow 3 to 5 minutes for each ½ inch of thickness.) Serve with Tomato Basil Butter Sauce. Garnish with basil leaves and squash slices. Serve with noodles, if desired. *Makes 4 servings*

TOMATO BASIL BUTTER SAUCE

4 tablespoons butter or margarine, softened, divided
1½ cups chopped seeded peeled tomatoes (about
    1 pound)
½ teaspoon sugar
1 clove garlic, minced
Salt and black pepper
1½ tablespoons very finely chopped fresh basil

Melt 1 tablespoon butter in a small skillet. Add tomato, sugar and garlic. Cook over medium-low heat, stirring frequently, until liquid evaporates and mixture thickens. Remove pan from heat; stir in remaining butter until mixture has a saucelike consistency. Season to taste with salt and pepper, then stir in basil. Makes about 1 cup.

Grilled Fish Steaks with
Tomato Basil Butter Sauce

Sensational SMOKED MEATS

SMOKE–COOKED BEEF RIBS

Three of these meaty beef back ribs make a meal. Because the ribs are so large, if you plan to cook more than 4 pounds, you may need to use a rib rack to hold them.

> **Wood chunks or chips for smoking**
> **4 to 6 pounds beef back ribs, cut in slabs of 3 to 4 ribs each**
> **Salt and black pepper**
> **1⅓ cups K.C. Masterpiece Barbecue Sauce**
> **Beer at room temperature *or* hot tap water**
> **Grilled Corn-on-the-Cob (optional) (page 84)**

Soak 4 wood chunks or several handfuls of wood chips in water; drain. Spread ribs on a baking sheet or tray; season with salt and pepper. Brush with half of sauce. Let stand at cool room temperature up to 30 minutes.

Arrange low Kingsford briquets on each side of a rectangular metal or foil drip pan. (Since the ribs have been brushed with sauce before cooking, low heat is needed to keep them moist.) Pour in beer to fill pan half full. Add soaked wood (all the chunks; part of the chips) to the fire.

Oil hot grid to help prevent sticking. Place ribs on grid, meaty side up, directly above drip pan. Smoke-cook ribs, on a covered grill, about 1 hour, brushing remaining sauce over ribs 2 or 3 times during cooking. If your grill has a thermometer, maintain a cooking temperature between 250°F to 275°F. Add a few more briquets after 30 minutes, or as necessary, to maintain a constant temperature. Add more soaked wood chips every 30 minutes, if necessary. Serve with Grilled Corn-on-the-Cob, if desired.

Makes 4 to 6 servings

Smoke-Cooked Beef Ribs and Grilled Corn-on-the-Cob (page 84)

POINTERS ON SMOKE-COOKING
IN A COVERED GRILL

- Our smoke-cooked recipes were developed for the covered grill. They may be easily adapted to a portable water smoker by following the grill manufacturer's guidelines for how much charcoal, wood and liquid to use. Because smoke-cooking in a water smoker is a longer process than in a covered barbecue, the food will take on a stronger smoky flavor.

- Hickory is the most popular aromatic hardwood. Its dense smoke imparts a rich, sweet flavor. But don't overdo it—too much smoke is overwhelming and turns food bitter. You can also flavor meat with mesquite, oak, pecan, grapevine clippings and fruit woods, such as peach or cherry. Don't use soft woods and evergreens, such as pine, cedar, spruce or fir. They leave a bitter-tasting pitch and resin that taints the food and coats the inside of the grill.

- Chunks, chips or twigs of hardwood may be purchased with barbecue supplies. Soak them in water first so they smoke rather than burn quickly. Because chunks burn slowly, you'll only need to add them to the coals in the beginning when you start smoke-cooking. Wood chips burn more quickly, so add some chips right before the meat is placed on the grill, then more during cooking.

- Before smoke-cooking, soak chips in water for 30 minutes; soak chunks up to 2 hours. This will cause them to smoke rather than to burst into flames. Be careful not to oversoak; water logged wood slows the cooking process.

- Start with about four wood chunks or several handfuls of chips (about 2 cups). As you become more experienced you can use more or less wood to suit your taste.

- Smoke-cooked foods stay moist because they cook in a smoky fog. Liquid, such as beer or water, is held in a drip pan to keep food moist and juicy.

- To enhance the wood-smoked flavor, add a fragrant herb or spice, or a peel from citrus fruit to the coals along with the soaked wood during the last 10 minutes of cooking. Aromatic possibilities include fresh rosemary, bay leaves, sage, ginger or garlic cloves.

- Cooking times are approximate. Cooking time is affected by the distance of the food from the coals, the size of the grill, the outdoor temperature and the size and temperature of the meat to be cooked.

- Use a meat thermometer to check when meat is done. The internal temperature of meat smoke-cooked on a covered grill can increase 5°F or more after it's removed from the grill. For best results, remove the meat just before it reaches the proper temperature.

SOY–GINGER SMOKED CHICKEN

Smoked foods taste so good that you may want to cook enough for several meals. Leftover chicken can be shredded and made into a delicious salad; leftover basting sauce can then be used as the salad dressing.

> **Wood chunks or chips for smoking**
> **Soy-Ginger Baste & Dressing (recipe follows)**
> **2 roasting chickens (each 3 to 4 pounds)**
> **Salt and black pepper**
> **10 to 12 thin slices fresh ginger**
> **Beer at room temperature**

Soak 4 wood chunks or several handfuls of chips in water; drain. Prepare Soy-Ginger Baste & Dressing.

Rinse chickens; pat dry with paper towels. Season with salt and pepper. Place 5 to 6 slices of ginger in cavity of each chicken. Tuck wings under back and tie legs together with cotton string. Brush Soy-Ginger Baste & Dressing on each chicken.

Arrange medium-low Kingsford briquets on each side of a rectangular metal or foil drip pan. Pour equal amounts of hot tap water and beer into the drip pan until pan is half full. Add soaked wood (all the chunks; part of the chips) to the fire.

Oil hot grid to help prevent sticking. Place chicken, breast side up on grid, directly above drip pan. Smoke-cook chicken, on a covered grill, 1½ to 2 hours until a meat thermometer inserted in the thigh registers 175° to 180°F or until the joints move easily and juices run clear when chicken is pierced. If your grill has a thermometer, maintain a cooking temperature of about 300°F. Add a few more briquets to both sides of the fire after 45 minutes to 1 hour, or as necessary, to maintain a constant temperature. At the same time, baste with more Soy-Ginger Baste & Dressing. Add more soaked chips every 45 minutes. *Makes 4 servings*

SOY–GINGER BASTE & DRESSING

> **1 cup vegetable oil**
> **2 tablespoons Oriental sesame oil**
> **⅓ cup seasoned (sweet) rice vinegar**
> **⅓ cup soy sauce**
> **2 tablespoons Dijon mustard**
> **1 tablespoon grated or minced fresh ginger**
> **½ to 1 teaspoon crushed red pepper flakes**

Whisk together all ingredients in a small bowl until blended. Makes about 2 cups.

SOUTHERN PORK BARBECUE

Slow cooking over low coals is the key to a great Southern barbecue. This is definitely not a quick-cooker—the pork needs 4 to 6 hours on a covered grill.

    1 boneless pork shoulder roast or Boston butt (about 5 pounds)
    Dan's Marinade & Moppin' Sauce (recipe follows)
4 cups hickory chips for smoking*
    K.C. Masterpiece Barbecue Sauce
    Cornmeal Griddle Cakes (page 80)
    Old-Time Coleslaw (page 80)
    Apple wedges for garnish

Place pork in a large heavy plastic bag. Add 1 cup of Dan's Marinade & Moppin' Sauce; close bag. Marinate in refrigerator 8 to 24 hours. Remove pork from marinade; discard marinade.

Soak hickory chips in water; drain. Arrange low Kingsford briquets on each side of a rectangular metal or foil drip pan. Pour in hot tap water to fill pan half full. Add some of the soaked chips to the fire.

Oil hot grid to help prevent sticking. Place pork on grid directly above drip pan. Smoke-cook pork, on a covered grill, 4 to 6 hours until a meat thermometer inserted in the thickest part registers 155°F and pork is very tender. Cook slowly over low coals. If your grill has a thermometer, maintain a cooking temperature of about 200°F. Add a few more briquets to both sides of the fire every hour, or as necessary, to maintain a constant temperature. Add more soaked hickory chips about every 30 minutes and baste with reserved moppin' sauce. Let pork stand 10 minutes before slicing. Heat K.C. Masterpiece Barbecue Sauce in a saucepan. Thinly slice pork and serve with barbecue sauce, Cornmeal Griddle Cakes and Old-Time Coleslaw. Garnish with apple wedges.   *Makes 10 to 12 servings*

*Due to the long cooking time, this recipe requires more hickory wood for smoking than is required in most of our recipes.

Note: For a Carolina-Style Chopped Pork Sandwich, chop the barbecued pork and heap onto the bottom of a hamburger bun. Pour on K.C. Masterpiece Barbecue Sauce, then top with coleslaw. Cover with top of bun.

DAN'S MARINADE & MOPPIN' SAUCE

    2 cups cider vinegar
1½ cups firmly packed dark brown sugar
    ¼ cup molasses
    6 cloves garlic, minced
    2 tablespoons ground red pepper
    2 tablespoons paprika
    2 tablespoons salt
    2 teaspoons black pepper

Stir together all ingredients in a small bowl until sugar is dissolved. Cover; refrigerate 4 hours or overnight to allow flavors to blend. Makes about 3½ cups.

continued on page 80

Southern Pork Barbecue

CORNMEAL GRIDDLE CAKES

2 cups yellow cornmeal
2 cups all-purpose flour
⅓ cup sugar
2 tablespoons baking powder
2 teaspoons salt
⅓ cup maple syrup
2 eggs
2 cups milk
½ cup vegetable oil
Butter or margarine

Combine cornmeal, flour, sugar, baking powder and salt in a large bowl. Combine maple syrup, eggs, milk and oil in a medium bowl. Add liquid ingredients to dry ingredients and stir just to blend. (Do not overmix; batter will be lumpy.)

Melt about 1 tablespoon butter in a large skillet; swirl to coat bottom of skillet. For each griddle cake, pour about ⅓ cup batter into skillet; cook until puffed and dry around edges. Turn and cook other side until golden brown. Repeat with remaining batter until all griddle cakes are made, adding more butter as needed. Griddle cakes can be kept warm in a low oven until serving, or reheated in the microwave. Makes about 20 griddle cakes.

OLD-TIME COLESLAW

2 heads green cabbage, shredded
3 large red apples, cored, chopped
⅔ cup sliced green onions
1½ cups mayonnaise
½ cup cider vinegar
¼ cup sugar
1 teaspoon salt
1 teaspoon black pepper
¼ to ½ teaspoon ground red pepper

Toss cabbage, apples and green onions in a large bowl. Mix remaining ingredients in a small bowl. Pour dressing over cabbage mixture; toss to coat. Cover and refrigerate until serving. Makes about 12 servings.

SMOKED TURKEY

A small turkey is perfect for family meals or informal gatherings. When buying a turkey, allow ¾ to 1 pound per person—leftovers make terrific sandwiches.

> **Wood chunks or chips for smoking**
> **1 turkey (8 to 14 pounds), thawed if frozen, neck**
> **and giblets removed**
> **1 lemon**
> **½ cup butter or margarine, melted**
> **⅓ cup finely chopped mixed fresh herbs***
> **2 cloves garlic, minced**
> **1 teaspoon Dijon mustard**
> **½ teaspoon salt**
> **½ teaspoon black pepper**
> **Fresh herbs for garnish**

Soak 4 to 6 wood chunks or several handfuls of wood chips in water; drain. Rinse turkey; pat dry with paper towels. Tuck wing tips under back and tie legs together. Squeeze 1½ tablespoons juice from lemon; mix with butter, chopped herbs, garlic, mustard, salt and pepper in a small bowl. Place remaining lemon in cavity of turkey.

Arrange medium-low Kingsford briquets on each side of a rectangular metal or foil drip pan. Pour in hot tap water to fill pan half full. Add soaked wood (all the chunks; part of the chips) to the fire.

Oil hot grid to help prevent sticking. Place turkey breast side up on grid, directly over drip pan. Smoke-cook turkey, on a covered grill, 11 to 14 minutes per pound until a meat thermometer inserted in the thigh registers 180°F or until joints move easily and juices run clear when turkey is pierced. Baste turkey three or four times with butter mixture during grilling. If your grill has a thermometer, maintain a cooking temperature of about 300°F. Add a few more briquets to both sides of the fire every 45 minutes to 1 hour, or as necessary, to maintain a constant temperature. Add more soaked wood chips every 30 to 45 minutes. Let turkey stand 10 to 20 minutes before slicing. Garnish with fresh herbs.

Makes 8 to 14 servings

* Substitute ½ teaspoon *each* dried thyme, oregano, rosemary, basil and rubbed sage *plus* 2 tablespoons finely chopped fresh parsley for the mixed fresh herbs.

Spectacular SIDE DISHES

GRILLED VEGETABLES WITH BALSAMIC VINAIGRETTE

Vegetables cut lengthwise, rather than crosswise, won't slip through the grid.

> 1 medium eggplant (about 1¼ pounds)
> 2 medium zucchini
> 2 to 3 medium yellow squash
> 2 medium red bell peppers
> ¾ cup olive oil
> ¼ cup balsamic vinegar
> 1 teaspoons salt
> ¼ teaspoon black pepper
> 1 clove garlic, minced
> 2 to 3 tablespoons finely chopped mixed fresh herbs
>   Herb sprigs for garnish

Trim, then slice eggplant, zucchini and yellow squash lengthwise into ¼- to ½-inch-thick slices. Core, seed and cut red peppers into 1-inch-wide strips. Place vegetables in a deep serving platter or wide shallow casserole. Combine oil, vinegar, salt, black pepper, garlic and chopped herbs in small bowl. Pour vinaigrette over vegetables; turn to coat. Let stand 30 minutes or longer. Lift vegetables from vinaigrette, leaving vinaigrette that doesn't cling to the vegetables in the dish.

Oil hot grid to help prevent sticking. Grill vegetables, on a covered grill, over medium Kingsford briquets, 8 to 16 minutes until fork-tender, turning once or twice. (Time will depend on the vegetable; eggplant takes the longest.) As vegetables are done, return them to the platter, then turn to coat with vinaigrette. (Or, cut eggplant, zucchini and yellow squash into cubes, then toss with red peppers and vinaigrette.) Garnish with herb sprigs. Serve warm or at room temperature.   *Makes 6 servings*

Grilled Vegetables with Balsamic Vinaigrette

GRILLED CORN SOUP

Grilled corn-on-the-cob is an all-time favorite, so grill-up extra, and turn it into a fabulous quick soup the next day.

4 ears grilled corn, husks removed
5 green onions
4 cups chicken broth, divided
Salt and black pepper

Cut kernels from cobs to make 2 to 2½ cups. Slice green onions, separating the white part from the green. Place corn, the white part of onions and 2 cups chicken broth in a blender or food processor; process until mixture is slightly lumpy. Place corn mixture in a large saucepan; add remaining chicken broth. Simmer gently 15 minutes. Stir in sliced green onion tops; season to taste with salt and pepper. *Makes 4 to 6 servings*

Grilled Corn-on-the-Cob: Turn back corn husks; do not remove. Remove silks with stiff brush; rinse corn under cold running water. Smooth husks back into position. Grill ears, on a covered grill, over medium-hot Kingsford briquets, about 25 minutes or until tender, turning corn often. Remove husks and serve.

GRILLED ZUCCHINI

3 medium zucchini
Seasonings: any combination of basil, oregano,
thyme, dill weed, lemon pepper, grated
Parmesan cheese, celery salt or garlic salt
2 to 3 tablespoons butter or margarine, softened

Cut zucchini lengthwise into halves. Sprinkle 3 halves with desired seasoning. Spread butter on remaining 3 halves. Place seasoned and buttered halves together; cut crosswise and wrap individual servings in heavy-duty foil, sealing edges tightly.

Grill zucchini, on an uncovered grill, over medium-hot Kingsford briquets, 15 to 20 minutes or until tender, turning often. *Makes 6 servings*

GARLIC MUSHROOMS

32 large fresh mushrooms
½ cup olive or vegetable oil
2 cloves garlic, minced

Remove stems from mushrooms; reserve caps. Combine oil and garlic in a medium bowl. Add mushroom caps; toss lightly to coat. Remove mushrooms with slotted spoon; place mushroom caps on piece of heavy-duty foil. Close foil over mushrooms, sealing edges tightly. Grill at edge of grid, over medium-hot Kingsford briquets, 10 to 15 minutes or until tender.
Makes 8 servings

RANCH PICNIC POTATO SALAD

6 medium potatoes (about 3½ pounds), cooked, peeled and sliced
½ cup chopped celery
¼ cup sliced green onions
2 tablespoons chopped parsley
¼ teaspoon salt
⅛ teaspoon black pepper
1 tablespoon Dijon mustard
1 cup prepared Hidden Valley Ranch Original Ranch Salad Dressing
2 hard cooked eggs, finely chopped
Paprika
Lettuce (optional)

Combine potatoes, celery, onions, parsley, salt and pepper in a large bowl. Stir mustard into salad dressing in a small bowl. Pour over potatoes; toss lightly to coat. Cover and refrigerate several hours. Sprinkle with eggs and paprika. Serve in lettuce-lined bowl, if desired.   *Makes 8 servings*

GRILLED EGGPLANT SANDWICHES

Cut in halves or quarters, these make terrific hors d'oeuvres.

1 eggplant (about 1¼ pounds)
Salt and black pepper
6 thin slices Provolone cheese
6 thin slices deli-style ham or mortadella
Fresh basil leaves (optional)
Olive oil

Cut eggplant into 12 (⅜-inch-thick) rounds; sprinkle both sides with salt and pepper. Top each of 6 eggplant slices with a slice of cheese, a slice of meat (fold or tear to fit) and a few basil leaves, if desired. Cover with a slice of eggplant. Brush one side with olive oil. Secure each sandwich with 2 or 3 toothpicks.

Oil hot grid to help prevent sticking. Grill eggplant oil side down, on a covered grill, over medium Kingsford briquets, 15 to 20 minutes. Halfway through cooking time, brush top with oil, then turn and continue grilling until eggplant is tender when pierced. (When turning, position sandwiches so toothpicks extend down between spaces in grid.) If eggplant starts to char before it's cooked through, move to a cooler part of the grill. Let sandwiches cool about 5 minutes, then cut into halves or quarters, if desired. Serve warm or at room temperature.   *Makes 6 sandwiches*

HONEY DIJON FRUIT SALAD

½ cup prepared Hidden Valley Ranch Honey Dijon
    Ranch Creamy Dressing
½ cup low-fat pineapple-flavored yogurt
¼ cup finely chopped fresh pineapple or drained
    canned crushed pineapple
1 teaspoon grated lemon peel
1 teaspoon lemon juice
4 cups assorted fresh fruit (grapes, berries, sliced
    apples, pears or bananas)
Lettuce leaves

Combine dressing, yogurt, pineapple, lemon peel and lemon juice in medium bowl. Arrange fruit on lettuce-lined serving plate or 4 individual plates. Serve dressing with salad. *Makes 4 servings*

APPLE−NUT SLAW

½ head green cabbage, shredded
1 cup shredded red cabbage
1 cup toasted walnuts*
2 red apples, sliced
1½ cups prepared Hidden Valley Ranch Reduced
    Calorie *or* Low Fat Original Ranch Salad
    Dressing

Combine all ingredients in a large bowl; toss gently to coat. Cover and refrigerate until ready to serve. *Makes 4 to 6 servings*

*To toast walnuts, spread in a single layer on a baking sheet. Toast in a preheated 350°F oven 8 to 10 minutes until very lightly browned.

RANCH THAI PEANUT DIP

½ cup sour cream
¼ cup crunchy peanut butter, unsalted
1 envelope (1.0 ounce) Hidden Valley Ranch
    Original Ranch Salad Dressing Mix
3 tablespoons milk
2 tablespoons lemon juice
2 tablespoons chopped unsalted peanuts
⅛ teaspoon ground red pepper

Combine all ingredients in a small bowl until well blended. Cover and refrigerate at least 1 hour to allow flavors to blend. Serve with assorted vegetables and warm chicken nuggets. *Makes about 1 cup*

*Top to bottom: Honey Dijon Fruit
Salad, Apple-Nut Slaw*

FIESTA RANCH BEAN DIP

1 envelope (1.0 ounce) Hidden Valley Ranch Fiesta
   Ranch Dip Mix
1 can (16 ounces) refried beans
½ pint (8 ounces) sour cream
1 can (7 ounces) diced green chilies, drained
   Shredded cheese, optional

Combine ingredients in a medium saucepan until well blended. Warm over medium heat until heated through, stirring occasionally. Pour into serving bowl; top with cheese. Serve with tortilla chips.   *Makes 3½ cups*

SOUTHWESTERN GUACAMOLE

1 cup mashed avocados (about 2 small)
¼ cup prepared Hidden Valley Ranch Taco Ranch
   Creamy Dressing

Combine avocado and dressing in a small bowl until blended. Serve with tortilla chips.   *Makes 1 cup*

CUCUMBER DILL DIP

2 cups prepared Hidden Valley Reduced Calorie
   Party Dip
1 cup chopped seeded peeled cucumber
1 tablespoon grated Parmesan cheese
¼ teaspoon dried dill weed

Combine all ingredients in a small bowl until well blended. Cover and refrigerate 1 to 2 hours to allow flavors to blend.   *Makes about 2½ cups*

MEXICAN–STYLE CORN SALAD

1 can (11 ounces) Mexican-style corn, drained
¼ cup sliced radishes
½ cup prepared Hidden Valley Ranch Taco Ranch
   Creamy Dressing

Combine all ingredients in a small bowl until blended. Cover and refrigerate until chilled.   *Makes 4 servings*

SANDWICHES

Grilling leftover beef, turkey, chicken, pork—even fish—can make terrific sandwiches with one of the following spreads or relish.

AIOLI

1 cup reduced-calorie or regular mayonnaise
4 cloves garlic, pressed
1 tablespoon Dijon mustard
1 tablespoon lemon juice or to taste

Combine ingredients in small bowl until well blended. Cover and refrigerate 1 to 2 hours to allow flavors to blend. Makes 1 cup.

GREEN CHILI MAYONNAISE

1 cup reduced-calorie or regular mayonnaise
1 can (7 ounces) chopped mild green chilies,
**   drained and patted dry with paper towels**
¼ cup chopped fresh cilantro
1 tablespoon lime juice or to taste
**   Salt to taste**

Combine all ingredients in a blender or food processor; process until well blended. Makes about 1¼ cups.

K.C. MASTERPIECE SPREAD

¼ cup K.C. Masterpiece Barbecue Sauce
¼ cup reduced-calorie or regular mayonnaise

Combine barbecue sauce and mayonnaise in a small bowl until smooth. Makes 1 cup.

RED RELISH

1 red bell pepper, quartered and seeded
1 large tomato, cut into halves, seeded and
**   squeezed to drain some juice**
2 tablespoons balsamic vinegar*
2 tablespoons chopped fresh basil
**   Salt and black pepper**

Grill bell pepper skin side down, on an uncovered grill, over medium Kingsford briquets, until skin starts to blister and peppers turn limp. Add tomato to grill two minutes after the pepper. Grill until tomato begins to turn limp. Remove from grill and let cool. Chop pepper and tomato; combine with remaining ingredients. Makes about 1⅓ cups.

*Substitute 1 tablespoon red wine vinegar *plus* ½ teaspoon sugar for the balsamic vinegar.

GRILLED PIZZA

A fun idea for parties, these pizzas are assembled on the grill. Because they're individual size, guests can make their own. Create your own combinations or follow the ideas given below.

> **2 loaves (1 pound each) frozen bread dough, thawed***
> **Olive oil**
> **K.C. Masterpiece Barbecue Sauce or pizza sauce**
> **Seasonings: finely chopped garlic and fresh or dried herbs**
> **Toppings: any combination of slivered ham, leftover shredded barbecued chicken and grilled vegetables, such as thinly sliced mushrooms, zucchini, yellow squash, bell peppers, eggplant, pitted olives, pineapple chunks, sliced tomatoes**
> **Salt and black pepper**
> **Cheese: any combination of shredded mozzarella, Provolone, Monterey Jack, grated Parmesan or crumbled feta**

Divide each loaf of dough into 4 balls. Roll on cornmeal or lightly floured surface and pat out dough to ¼-inch thickness to make small circles. Brush each circle with oil.

Arrange hot Kingsford briquets on one side of the grill. Oil hot grid to help prevent sticking. Vegetables, such as mushrooms, zucchini, yellow squash, bell peppers and eggplant need to be grilled until tender before using them as toppings. (See tip below.)

Place 4 circles directly above medium Kingsford briquets. (The dough will not fall through the grid.) Grill circles, on an uncovered grill, until dough starts to bubble in spots on the top and the bottom gets lightly browned. Turn over using tongs. Continue to grill until the other side is lightly browned, then move the crusts to the cool part of the grill.

Brush each crust lightly with barbecue sauce, top with garlic and herbs, then meat or vegetables. Season with salt and pepper, then top with cheese. Cover pizzas and grill, about 5 minutes until cheese melts, bottom of crust is crisp and pizza looks done. Repeat with remaining dough.

Makes 8 individual pizzas

Note: Vegetables such as mushrooms, zucchini, yellow squash, bell peppers and eggplant should be grilled before adding to pizza. If used raw, they will not have enough time to cook through. To grill, thread cut-up vegetables on skewers. Brush lightly with oil. Grill vegetables, on an uncovered grill, over hot Kingsford briquets, until tender, turning frequently. Or place a piece of wire mesh on the grid, such as the type used for screen doors, to keep the vegetables from slipping through the grid.

Ham & Pineapple Pizza: Brush crust lightly with K.C. Masterpiece Barbecue Sauce and top with minced garlic, slivered ham, grilled bell peppers, pineapple chunks and shredded mozzarella or Monterey Jack cheese.

Veggie-Herb Pizza: Brush crust lightly with pizza sauce and top with finely chopped basil, minced garlic and grilled mushrooms, zucchini and green bell pepper. Sprinkle with grated Parmesan cheese.

Tomato-Feta Pizza: Top crust with minced garlic and crumbled dried herbs or minced fresh herbs, such as oregano, rosemary and basil. Top with chopped fresh tomato, slivered red onion and coarsely chopped olives. Sprinkle with grated Parmesan cheese and crumbled feta cheese.

*Substitute your favorite pizza crust recipe. Dough for 1 large pizza will make 4 individual ones.

SKEWERED VEGETABLES

> 2 medium zucchini, cut lengthwise into halves, then
>   cut into 1-inch slices
> 8 pearl onions, cut into halves
> ½ red bell pepper, cut into 1-inch pieces
> 8 fresh medium mushrooms (optional)
> 16 lemon slices
> 2 tablespoons butter or margarine, melted
> Salt and black pepper

Place zucchini, onions and red pepper in a medium saucepan with enough water to cover. Bring to a boil; cover and continue boiling for 1 minute. Remove with slotted spoon and drain. Alternately thread zucchini, onions, red pepper, mushrooms and lemon slices onto 8 metal or bamboo skewers. (Soak bamboo skewers in water at least 20 minutes to keep them from burning.)

Oil hot grid to help prevent sticking. Brush vegetables with butter. Grill vegetables, on a covered grill, over medium-hot Kingsford briquets, 6 minutes or until tender, carefully turning skewers and brushing with butter once. Season to taste with salt and pepper. Serve immediately.

Makes 8 servings

INDEX

METRIC CONVERSION CHART

VOLUME MEASUREMENTS (dry)

⅛ teaspoon = 0.5 mL
¼ teaspoon = 1 mL
½ teaspoon = 2 mL
¾ teaspoon = 4 mL
1 teaspoon = 5 mL
1 tablespoon = 15 mL
2 tablespoons = 30 mL
¼ cup = 60 mL
⅓ cup = 75 mL
½ cup = 125 mL
⅔ cup = 150 mL
¾ cup = 175 mL
1 cup = 250 mL
2 cups = 1 pint = 500 mL
3 cups = 750 mL
4 cups = 1 quart = 1 L

VOLUME MEASUREMENTS (fluid)

1 fluid ounce (2 tablespoons) = 30 mL
4 fluid ounces (½ cup) = 125 mL
8 fluid ounces (1 cup) = 250 mL
12 fluid ounces (1½ cups) = 375 mL
16 fluid ounces (2 cups) = 500 mL

WEIGHTS (mass)

½ ounce = 15 g
1 ounce = 30 g
3 ounces = 90 g
4 ounces = 120 g
8 ounces = 225 g
10 ounces = 285 g
12 ounces = 360 g
16 ounces = 1 pound = 450 g

DIMENSIONS

1/16 inch = 2 mm
⅛ inch = 3 mm
¼ inch = 6 mm
½ inch = 1.5 cm
¾ inch = 2 cm
1 inch = 2.5 cm

OVEN TEMPERATURES

250°F = 120°C
275°F = 140°C
300°F = 150°C
325°F = 160°C
350°F = 180°C
375°F = 190°C
400°F = 200°C
425°F = 220°C
450°F = 230°C

BAKING PAN SIZES

Utensil	Size in Inches/Quarts	Metric Volume	Size in Centimeters
Baking or Cake Pan (square or rectangular)	8×8×2	2 L	20×20×5
	9×9×2	2.5 L	23×23×5
	12×8×2	3 L	30×20×5
	13×9×2	3.5 L	33×23×5
Loaf Pan	8×4×3	1.5 L	20×10×7
	9×5×3	2 L	23×13×7
Round Layer Cake Pan	8×1½	1.2 L	20×4
	9×1½	1.5 L	23×4
Pie Plate	8×1¼	750 mL	20×3
	9×1¼	1 L	23×3
Baking Dish or Casserole	1 quart	1 L	—
	1½ quart	1.5 L	—
	2 quart	2 L	—